The Road Leads Home

Inspiring Stories from the Texas Hill Country

This book was written for the express purpose of conveying the love and mercy of Jesus Christ. The statements in this book are substantially true; however, names and minor details have been changed to protect people and situations from accusation or incrimination.

Published in Beaverton, Oregon, by Good Catch Publishing.
www.goodcatchpublishing.com
V1.1

Printed in the United States of America

Table of Contents

Dedication

"We cannot put off living until we are ready.
The most salient characteristic of life is its coerciveness:
It is always urgent, 'here and now,' without any possible
postponement. Life is fired at us pointblank."

– Jose Ortegay Gasset

Pain, suffering, humiliation, failure and defeat are all a part of this experience called life. It can catch us unprepared. It can steal our sense of well-being. It can sap us of the strength to continue on. You may have come to the point of wondering if there is any hope or if anyone cares. The answer might surprise you. This book is for you!

Acknowledgements

I would like to thank RJ Dugone for his vision for this book and Nina Pena for her hard work in making it a reality. And to the people of BC, thank you for your boldness and vulnerability in sharing your personal stories.

This book would not have been published without the amazing efforts of our project manager and editor, Hayley Pandolph. Her untiring resolve pushed this project forward and turned it into a stunning victory. Thank you for your great fortitude and diligence. Deep thanks to our incredible editor in chief, Michelle Cuthrell, and executive editor, Jen Genovesi, for all the amazing work they do. I would also like to thank our invaluable proofreader, Melody Davis, for the focus and energy she has put into perfecting our words.

Lastly, I want to extend our gratitude to the creative and very talented Jenny Randle, who designed the beautiful cover for *The Road Leads Home: Inspiring Stories from the Texas Hill Country*.

Daren Lindley
President and CEO
Good Catch Publishing

The book you are about to read
is a compilation of authentic life stories.
The facts are true, and the events are real.
These storytellers have dealt with crisis, tragedy, abuse
and neglect and have shared their most private moments,
mess-ups and hang-ups in order for others to learn and
grow from them. In order to protect the identities of those
involved in their pasts, the names and details of some
storytellers have been withheld or changed.

Introduction

What do you do when life is careening out of control? When addiction has overtaken you or abuse chained you with fear? Is depression escapable? Will relationships ever be healthy again? Are we destined to dissolve into an abyss of sorrow? Or will the sunlight of happiness ever return?

Your life really can change. It is possible to become a new person. The seven stories you are about to read prove positively that people right here in our town have stopped dying and started living. Whether you've been beaten by abuse, broken promises, shattered dreams or suffocating addictions, the resounding answer is: "Yes! You can become a new person." The potential to break free from gloom and into a bright future awaits.

Expect inspiration, hope and transformation! As you walk with the people from our very own city through the pages of this book, you will not only find riveting accounts of their hardships, you will learn the secrets that brought about their breakthroughs. These people are no longer living in the shadows of yesterday; they are thriving with a sense of mission and purpose TODAY. May these stories inspire you to do the same.

For the Long Haul

The Story of Joshua

Written by Douglas Abbott

I couldn't stop thinking about the gun in my roommate's nightstand. I had seen Joe pull it out on occasion. Whenever he did, he was careful to remove the clip and pop the round out of the chamber, so I knew he kept it loaded.

It wasn't natural for me to think about suicide. I had always been an optimist, carrying myself with a sunny disposition. But now, all I could see was total defeat. When I looked in the mirror, I no longer saw a kind, well-spoken gentleman. I saw someone who had lost control over his own behavior, his own life. What had begun many years before as a secret indulgence had completely engulfed me. I felt a shame so strong that it was like I was burning.

It was simple: If I couldn't win this battle, nothing was left. All my goals and everything I looked forward to in life hinged on my beating this thing. But instead, I had been beaten by it again and again.

Maybe it was time to pull the plug. But there was no hurry. Joe's gun wasn't going anywhere.

My siblings and I grew up in college housing. After my father earned his master's degree, he went to work while my mother pursued her degree. All this took years to accomplish, so my siblings and I learned to look after ourselves, which wasn't too difficult on campus. I recall spending many entire days at the pool.

My father's specialty was athletics. He celebrated the masculine ideal of physical strength and prowess, boldness and unflinching confidence. I had none of these things. By any objective standard, I was effeminate. When my unusual sensitivity earned me a spot in my elementary school musical at an early age, it seemed to drive a wedge between me and the rest of my family. Most significantly, I was at odds with my father. I could literally *feel* his distaste for my effeminate mannerisms and my lack of enthusiasm for sports. I felt like an outsider. In retrospect, I believe they simply didn't know what to make of me.

I wasn't always so sure myself.

However, it wasn't just my father I had to worry about. Most of the people in our small community were just like him. So I learned to move and speak in classically masculine ways, and I pushed myself into sports. Dad would have preferred for me to go out for all the school sports, but perhaps understanding my own limitations, I concentrated on excelling in one — basketball.

But it wasn't enough. One day, as I walked home from school, I was accosted by a group of my peers who proceeded to needle me about my former effeminate ways.

"Here's the cheerleader!" they jeered.

I actually believed I could reason with them. "No, I'm not. That's been a long time ago now. Where have you been?"

The ringleader was undeterred. "No, see, your father told us all about you in gym class!" And they went off in gales of laughter.

My father came home and found me on the couch in a fetal position.

"What's the matter with you?" he said almost flippantly.

I exploded at him. "Why don't you ask your gym class?" I screamed. "You told them I was a cheerleader!"

My father overlooked my disrespectful tone and explained that he had used me as an example of how people should be themselves, go with their individuality.

But I was inconsolable. In the first place, I didn't quite believe him. In the second place, even if he was telling me the truth, I thought this was the dumbest reason he could have come up with for saying such a thing to his entire class.

The disclosure was all the worse because it was basically true. He had made light of a side of me I was ashamed of and had attempted to eliminate from my being. I thought my father secretly disliked me. Fortunately, I stayed afloat by virtue of my natural optimism, paired with a robust sense of humor. Additionally, I had the support and friendship of my brother, Lucas, who was one year younger and the only member of my family I felt accepted by.

When I was in the sixth grade, my parents hosted a family get-together. My uncle Frank's family was passing through and descended on our house for the evening. After a sumptuous dinner and an evening of socializing, the children (eight of us) were sent to our sleeping quarters.

My room was suddenly bursting at the seams. Even the floor was covered with boys draped in blankets. As everyone began to drift off to sleep, I lay wide awake. One of my cousins, José, was lying next to me.

"You want to have some fun?" José whispered, realizing I was as sleepless as he was.

"Sure!" I said. We joined our blankets together and employed flashlights as we embarked on a series of experimental games under the covers.

I didn't understand the nature of what we were doing. I sensed no danger. My feelings of attraction toward other males had been going on for some time, though I hadn't thought much about it. Nor had I spent any time examining what effect may have been produced by my early exposure to pornography (my friends often had magazines), my emotional estrangement from my own family or even my personality and physical characteristics. Any of these may have been factors in the path I chose. However, all I was aware of at the time was that I was being presented with an opportunity for companionship and intimacy, which I craved. Little did I know that getting close to José would open a floodgate of emotions and powerful attractions.

I began initiating physical contact with other boys at school. I imagine most of them were simply experimenting, but I had gone beyond experimentation. My aim was deliberate and true. I had found a source of comfort and acceptance that was so strong I couldn't bring myself to abandon it, even after I sensed a trap.

Sometime after my experience with José, I made friends with a classmate, Bobby. The two of us started a physical relationship that lasted all through high school. Neither of us would have cared to call it a relationship, but it remained constant as we continued to seek each other out. By the time my arrangement with Bobby became a regular thing, I felt misgivings. However, the trap was already set. I was fully invested emotionally and physically. Ironically, the thing I had been drawn into by my desire for intimacy ended up becoming an empty, selfish pursuit for me.

To make matters worse, the sexual rabbit trail I had gone down reinforced itself through fantasy, repetition, my use of pornography and, eventually, the failure of alternatives. During high school, I tried dating, but I noticed with dismay that my body failed to respond when I was with women. This brought me into a profound conflict. At my core, I didn't want to be attracted to men. I wanted a wife and children. I prayed often for a family. But that dream seemed to be out of reach.

I approached my high school graduation with an ambition to become an entertainer. I had always enjoyed sitcoms, film, music and drama, and I had been involved in theater at school for years and had even won awards. I wanted a career in show business, but I had resigned myself to a political science major (with a fallback teaching degree), partly in deference to my parents' counsel and partly because it was more practical than a degree in theater. When the time came, however, I chose theater/education and moved 800 miles away to begin my studies at a state university in Texas.

As I settled into college life, I continued my effort to redirect my sexuality. I was emotionally attracted to women and hoped that, by dating, I could help the physical component along.

I took a job as an aide in a psychiatric hospital working directly with mental patients. I began dating my supervisor, Aliena, an attractive woman. However, my body failed to respond to her sexually, and I resolved to end the affair before she discovered my secret. I planned to break it off with her after our next date.

The evening of our final outing, we attended a concert, after which she drove me to my car to drop me off. As we were getting out of the car, we were approached by an unkempt, heavily intoxicated man. His speech was angry and slurred. I knew instantly from Aliena's subdued response that she was in a relationship with this man.

Before I could collect my thoughts, the man took a swing at me, then at Aliena. Police swarmed the scene almost immediately, and I ran from the area. For some reason, the police made no issue of the assault, and Aliena and the guy went home together. The next time I saw her, she was wearing sunglasses to conceal a black eye.

To me, the incident represented a failure on my part. I felt shame over it for many years to come. It was not simply a moral failure; my choice to flee the scene rather than defend Aliena was proof to me that I was something less than a man. The pronouncement from the mirror was that I could never be a proper husband to a woman.

I put in my notice at the psychiatric hospital.

After my first year of college, I decided to stay and work through the summer. I shared an apartment with a theater major who was openly gay. He was a good friend and a good roommate. I saw that he and his partner had what looked like a good relationship (though his partner was gone for most of the summer studying). However, I still didn't feel that it was right for me. It wasn't something I wanted to pursue.

Later that summer, a friend invited me to accompany him to a service at his church, and I accepted. When the evening came, I enjoyed every part of it, including the music and the sermon, which was taken from the book of Romans: "However, to the one who does not work but trusts God who justifies the ungodly, their faith is credited as righteousness" (Romans 4:5).

I had always believed my standing with God was

directly related to my conduct. The pastor's words put me back in my seat. I had never understood the concept of unconditional forgiveness, and at no time in my life had I ever felt a greater need for it.

When I examined my life, I didn't look much different from unbelievers. I had an ongoing love affair with pornography that sometimes spilled over into anonymous encounters. I was afflicted with wanderlust. Most recently, my indecision had cost a woman a beating.

It shouldn't have felt like I was doing anything new or different when I raised my hand in response to the pastor's invitation to publicly accept Jesus. I had been raised Catholic and had long before embraced the core faith shared by Catholics and Protestants: that Jesus is the son of God, crucified for our sins and resurrected from the dead. I believed in the act of confession and the need for submission to God. In fact, I had been a devout Catholic for many years. Even as I struggled with an ongoing appetite for pornography, promiscuous behavior and other moral failures, I held onto my faith. In my darkest hour, I continued to attend Mass, deriving enormous comfort from the solemnity and quiet of the cathedral.

However, something undoubtedly changed that evening. After I answered the invitation, the pastor invited us to meet with members of the church for a follow-up. That was how I ended up in a small classroom in the back of the church telling my story to two men I had just met. Nothing of any great significance stood out about our meeting. Much of what we discussed is gone from my memory. But when I got home at the end of the night, I was grinning from ear to ear. I felt a great peace and knew that I was saved by a God who loved me. In that moment, I knew I was going to heaven.

Somehow, during all the years I attended Mass, my understanding was that my conduct would determine my eternal destination (heaven or hell) — a stipulation that left me in a bad spot, since I was in the middle of an unresolved struggle with homosexuality and porn addiction. But somehow, things had switched over to a different footing. It was as though God told me, *You are mine*. It was a title transfer, an overarching proclamation that couldn't be undone by my personal failings.

It wasn't as though I had changed my views about homosexuality. However, a distinctive change had occurred. Before, it was as if I had to choose between being accepted by Jesus or having struggles with homosexuality. Now I had internalized the fact that Jesus died for all my sins, even those I continued to deal with. In a paradoxical way, this colossal show of grace from God would be the key to change for me.

After that night, I transferred my membership from the Catholic church to this new non-denominational church. I gained a mentor in Tony, one of the men I had spoken with after the service. Tony was the worship leader and also a professional photographer. Soon, I was tagging along with him on photo shoots and soaking up his counsel. I was growing like a weed because of the fellowship I had found with Tony and others at the church. Everyone was eager to answer the many questions I had about Christianity. My life was suddenly full of vibrant activity with new church friends. Somehow the sermons I heard (though they covered the same material I had listened to almost every week of my life) were like jets of fire coming from the pulpit. As for my sexual struggles, I made them the subject of special, fervent prayer and trusted that God would walk me through all of it.

My family was profoundly unhappy with my departure from Catholicism. When I went home for the Christmas holiday, my mother wept, and my father told me, "When you're in my house, you'll attend Mass." Even my siblings were put out with me. It was as if I had renounced God.

I was shattered. I felt betrayed by my family and let down by God. I couldn't believe it was happening.

The rejection of my family affected me so deeply that it became a deal breaker. I stopped attending the non-denominational church and blamed them for my turmoil — as though they could somehow have known or been responsible for the reaction of my family. I resumed attending Mass, but my heart wasn't in it.

I had since returned to work for the psychiatric hospital, and I got word of new job openings with our parent company in Hawaii. Several friends I knew from both work and school had heard about the openings as well. Four of us applied and were hired. We saved up our money and, within a few months, quit school and moved to Hawaii.

During the flight, as I sat in coach flipping through a magazine, I came across an article about Hawaii in which the author discussed how many people moved to Hawaii thinking they were going to find paradise when they were really running away from something on the mainland. The article hit so close to home that I was angry all over again.

For some time after arriving in Hawaii, I thought I *was* in paradise. I made phenomenal money and enjoyed the tropical environment with my friends. The four of us shared an apartment and worked together at the hospital, which was brand-new. I resumed smoking pot, which I had first used in high school.

I mounted a renewed effort to rehabilitate myself sexually. There were many attractive women around, and it wasn't long before I noticed a girl making eyes at me while we were both retrieving our mail at my apartment building. Tess was quiet and pretty, and after some flirting in both directions, I asked her out.

When we got together for the first time, she was sporting a new shiner. Her husband, who had given it to her, had just moved back to the mainland. Our relationship only lasted a couple of months.

My flight from God did not produce good results in my life. My fixation on pornography grew, and in spite of my efforts to re-channel my sex drive, I was caught up in the pursuit of same-sex affairs — now brief, anonymous and growing in frequency.

What had begun as a grand adventure grew stale, and I felt isolated on the islands. I could find no rest. A year after I went to Hawaii, I quit my job at the psychiatric hospital and moved to New York. I signed on with a modeling agency and, while pursuing work along those lines, took a job at a Doubleday bookstore in Manhattan.

It was a random, disjointed time in my life. New York was rougher than I had imagined. I found myself disenchanted and stalled in my efforts to immerse myself in the theater scene in the city.

About the time my metropolitan adventure was fizzling out, I ran into a group of old friends from Texas, including Aliena, my one-time supervisor and romantic interest at the psychiatric hospital. After hanging out with them for a week, I decided to move back to Texas and resume my schooling.

Back on campus, I changed my major to phys ed and took two part-time jobs, working for a funeral home and driving a bus. I put a semester of school behind me. In spite of all the ways I had been avoiding God, I was concerned about my standing with him, particularly my forbidden indulgences, which I was still trying to stamp out of my life. Except for some drinking and pot smoking, I was doing fairly well, meaning I wasn't visiting adult bookstores or pursuing affairs. None of my wanderings had managed to extinguish my conscience. Whenever I failed in this troubling area, I was thrown into fresh turmoil.

After another semester, I traveled back home for Christmas break with an old friend, who had just completed his first semester of college. Luis and I hung out over the break, splitting our time between his family's house and mine.

Sometime during the break, Luis dedicated his life to Christ. The way the whole thing was described pointed to something extravagant.

"I just want you to know," Luis told me, "I've committed my life to Christ because you always used to tell me to trust him."

I couldn't figure for a second how it was possible for me to inspire anyone. I had been stagnating for more than a year, in full flight from God. But there it was. And somehow, Luis managed to help me back to my feet again. I caught the spark of his newborn enthusiasm, and before I had even left again for the spring semester, I prayed to God: *I'm coming back, Lord.*

And I meant it. As soon as I got back to campus, I plunged back into church life with gusto, attending Mass and also services at the same non-denominational church I'd attended before. I resumed my friendship with Tony, who had mentored me before, and began spending a great deal of time with him and his wife.

For reasons I don't remember, I also reached out to Campus Crusade for Christ. Other than spiritual growth, I'm not sure what I expected to find at CCC, but I encountered much more.

I was soon attending frequent Bible studies and, later, leading Bible studies with newer members. My life was suddenly filled with godly friends, activities and fulfillment I never knew possible. Some of my new friends chose me to be best man at their weddings, and many became lifelong friends.

Because of the spiritual growth spurt that was happening, I found that my sex issues had become vastly more manageable. I was completely celibate and only occasionally reached for pornography.

"I want to come on staff with Campus Crusade," I announced to my mentor, Dan. We were sipping coffee at the close of a marathon Bible study.

"Great!" Dan replied heartily. "When will you graduate?"

"I don't want to wait that long. I just want to quit school and start straight away."

Dan fidgeted a bit. "Well, it doesn't work that way. You have to have a degree."

So I went in to see my advisor.

"I want to get my degree as soon as possible," I told him. "I just need to graduate."

"Well, you have more theater credits than anything else," he said, consulting a printout. "Keep taking theater classes and you're not far off."

So I declared a theater major and filled out the application with CCC. While this was going on, the issue of my private struggle continued to come up. I found a question on the CCC application about struggles with sin. Then, Tony's wife, Judy, told him God had told her in a dream that I struggled with homosexuality. I didn't receive all this as criticism, but as an indication God was healing me.

Thus, I was bewildered when, after two uneventful years, I stumbled again. It was an unmemorable 60-second encounter with a stranger, but it carried the force of a bludgeon.

I had considered my struggle behind me, but now I was thrown into despondency and began contemplating suicide. I spent a morbid amount of time thinking about the revolver my roommate, Joe, kept in his nightstand. Sometimes, I imagined taking it out, thumbing off the safety and putting the barrel to my temple. Other times I thought about putting it in my mouth. All the scenarios seemed like an improvement over my current circumstances.

Death seemed like a reasonable outcome for me. I felt like a slave to my lusts, completely unworthy of the love God had lavished on me. Furthermore, this issue of mine was standing in the way of everything I wanted out of life — marriage, self-respect, a ministry of my own. Of all the problems I might have gotten shackled with, this one was a doozy — and apparently indestructible.

It was one time when my genius for running away actually helped me. While I was waiting for Campus Crusade to get back to me, I heard from a friend about a teaching opportunity in a town two hours away. By this time, I had received my degree and felt hesitant about getting accepted on staff with CCC. They had told me an ongoing struggle with sin would preclude employment. I was carrying around a strange mixture of thoughts.

On the one hand, I felt God was speaking clearly to

me, through others' dreams and all variety of things. On the other hand, my stumble had left me in ruins emotionally. Hence, when the opportunity for a move and a fresh start presented itself, I jumped on it.

That's how I ended up teaching high school theater. After I arrived there, I began attending a church in town and doing volunteer work with the youth — co-leading Bible studies, coordinating activities and putting together the newsletter.

I was enjoying many positive experiences, but I was still searching — or perhaps running.

In 1989, I auditioned for an acting school in New York and was accepted. However, my indecision was becoming almost a comedy of errors. After arriving in New York, I was so intimidated by the professional thespian environment (arguably the theater capital of the world) that I backed out of my enrollment, found some Christian roommates and took a teaching job at a Christian school.

I sought the help of a Christian counselor who specialized in "same-sex attraction." Joni saw me for two years, but at the end of them, she was blunt: "Your problem isn't homosexuality," she said. "You have to learn how to listen to what God is saying to you 24/7, otherwise you're going to keep stumbling. I can't help you anymore. You already know everything you need to know. You have to put it into practice."

For the next three years, I kept running and filling my life with random things. I worked mediocre jobs. I had one relationship with a woman who had two boys and with whom I discussed marriage. But it wasn't to be. Nothing could stick to me.

The high point of these years was my involvement with a Christian theater company in Manhattan. The owners, a husband and wife team, both had strong personal faith, compelling life stories and cared deeply about their work. I enjoyed an affectionate camaraderie with the other actors and crew, worked jobs on the side and acted with the company as much as I could. I was delighted when I got a role on a touring production of *Don Quixote*. I was traveling all over the country, getting paid to act. It was a dream come true.

All the while, my private life was like a cord tightening around my neck. I could see myself changing for the worse. My Christian walk collected dust on the shelf, while my secret indulgences overtook me.

Finally, I came to my senses and realized that if I didn't deal squarely with my lust, it would consume me. I would give in to a gay identity and capitulate completely to the whole lifestyle. I was terrified.

It was time to leave New York City.

I learned about an organization called Exodus, which oversaw programs for same-sex attraction across the country. I chose one in Wichita, Kansas, called Freedom At Last. Some of the program requirements didn't make sense to me, but I felt a powerful motivation just the same. I agreed with the premise of the program — that homosexuality is a sin but that people can change. That, in fact, God stood ready to help anyone wanting to change. I sensed God telling me to go through with this. More than once, an otherworldly assurance took hold of me: *This is it. I'm going to make it. Something good is going to happen.*

So I enrolled in the program and began attending another church, which sponsored our program. As I met the people there, I was astounded at how accepting they were of me. Not only had I disclosed my struggles to these virtual strangers, I must have seemed outlandish to them — a stage actor from New York City — now being embraced by a collection of small-town conservative Christians. Their acceptance was crucial. I was going to make it.

My schedule was full. There were meetings and church services and Bible studies — a full year of prayer and fellowship. Around the time I completed the program, I accepted a job as an assistant to the principal of an elementary school with the Wichita School District. I made friends with a married Christian man named Kyle, who was a teacher at the school where I was working. He and his wife, Dodi, regularly took in Christian boarders to disciple them. Just as I was graduating from FAL, Kyle's boarder moved out, and he invited me to take the room.

One evening at Kyle's, I was praying for direction when I suddenly felt sure God was telling me to go to work for FAL. But how was I going to carry that out? The only guarantee I had was that the staff would permit me to show up and volunteer my time organizing files and who knew what else. However, my superiors at church and even my friends sounded enthusiastic about it. I spoke to Monty, who had been my house leader at FAL.

"God is telling me to go to work at the program," I told him over coffee.

Monty started laughing.

"What's so funny?" I said.

"You're going to have a job waiting for you," he said, chuckling. "I just resigned as house leader. Matt's going to make you the house leader. You just watch!"

And that is exactly what the director of FAL did. I started on as house leader in early 1997. The position came with room and board and a very small stipend. It wasn't really enough to live on. However, in a bizarre turn of events, I continually ran into people at church or elsewhere who would tell me, "God told me I'm supposed to give you some money each month" or "God told me to take you shopping for clothes today." I had everything I needed. I had truly landed in an amazing church.

As house leader, I met with each resident once a week, attended meetings and had various administrative responsibilities. Over the first year, FAL grew from one house into three houses — two for men, one for women. Once they were up and running, I was asked to become the ministry director overseeing the spiritual life of all three houses. I also spoke at regional conferences and outreaches at local churches.

It was an incredible time of growth in my life and ministry. I bought a house in Wichita and, in 2000, was ordained as a minister by Faith Community Church. This was a sort of honorary ordination but also a practical outgrowth. As the pastor of FCC told me, "You've been doing the work of a pastor, so we're presenting you with credentials. Congratulations!"

During my time at FAL, I was frequently broke, at the edge of my endurance and always dealing with difficult situations. Many of the men I shepherded continued to succumb to temptation while they were in our program. One committed suicide, after which his mother and sister blamed me in the midst of their anguish. But ironically, I still consider it one of the very best times in my life.

In 2002, I moved to Austin to help my old friend Tony (from my college days) establish a residential ministry much like FAL. For many reasons, including the lack of demand for a residential program, we weren't able to get it off the ground. However, I stayed in Austin, joined North Austin Christian Church and began volunteering with the church youth. For income, I worked at a local high school teaching life skills to special-needs students.

I moved to Leander, Texas, in 2005, to help NACC establish a new church there. I had been working with the church in Austin for three years and was eager to help my pastors establish the Leander church, which we called Believers Church.

It has been a pleasure to help others who have faced difficult moral struggles, as I have. Most of my church mates are not surprised by anyone's failings, perhaps because they have not completely forgotten their own.

Sometime after my 40th birthday, my longtime mentor,

Tony, came alongside to offer some advice. He knew I had wanted for many years to be married.

"Josh, you're going to have to put yourself out there socially. It's not going to happen the way it might have when you were in college."

So I subscribed to e-Harmony and told trusted friends that I wanted to go on dates (even blind dates). This went on for six months or perhaps a year. Then a college friend Layne called me.

"Josh, how do feel about coming to San Antonio to meet a friend of mine? Nora is single, Christian and unattached. We can do a double date."

I was somewhat gun-shy. I had been on dates where, after disclosing my past struggles with homosexuality, I was told by my female companion, "Well, we're dead in the water. When you're gay, you're gay."

So when Layne proposed the double date, I was forthright: "Make sure she knows about my past."

Layne did as I asked, and Nora's response was, "We all have a past."

Nora is gentle and non-judgmental, with a wonderful laugh and captivating eyes. There is a quiet, unimposing way about her. Nora and I discussed all the contentious issues, but we both felt confident that God wanted us to find each other. Six months later, we were standing at the altar together.

I purposely postponed physical contact with Nora, both for the sake of purity and because I firmly resolved to trust God to work out all the obstacles I had encountered with women in the past. We went into marriage blindly in this regard, in utter faith.

It was the right thing to do. In late 2008, Nora and I welcomed our newborn son, Seth, into the world. In many ways, this now 6-year-old boy is the walking, talking proof of God's love and healing power.

I have had occasion recently to correspond with a young man named Richard, who is serving a term in federal prison for drug possession. During his time of searching, we began exchanging letters and e-mails. When he gave his life to Christ, I was, of course, delighted. But I knew he would need much encouragement for the difficulties ahead of him. One letter I sent him is like an echo of things my own mentors often told me.

> I know it is tempting to see your forthcoming release as a liberation. And it is. But I hope you will see that your choices immediately afterward are the pivotal issue. Not so much your mistakes, but your response to them. I'm speaking from personal experience here.
>
> God loves you and has a fantastic plan for your life. None of your mistakes can change that. If he died for you while you were still a sinner, why, just because you sin, would he stop loving you now that you're his son? I'm not saying it's fine to do as you please. I'm saying you must never forget that he's in this with you for the long haul. Never stop calling out to him! He will always be there for you.

Whenever I forget it, I look at Seth, remember God's goodness and smile.

Truth Triumphs

The Story of Mia

Written by Arlene Showalter

"Detective Smith, FBI." The man's lips stretched horizontal as he flashed his badge. "Please come with me, ma'am."

I followed in his somber wake as he led me to a small room, carrying my youngest while the older two clung to my clothes. *I hope this doesn't take long. Mom and Dad will be waiting for us.*

The door snapped shut. "You have anything explosive in your bag, ma'am?"

My mind and thoughts remained blank.

"Hairspray? Anything?"

I shook my head. *My bag? Explosives?* Our scramble from the airplane in Dallas flashed through my mind. *Smoke. Emergency exit. Hurry, hurry, hurry.*

"I don't understand."

"We traced an explosive to your bag. Please sit down. This could take some time."

As a child, life delivered peaceful contentment and tranquility. The youngest in a large family, most of my siblings had moved out of the house and on with their lives by the time I came along in our quaint Midwestern town.

"Can I go to Vacation Bible School?" I asked my parents when I was 6.

"Where, dear?"

"The church on the corner. They have a big sign out front. Can I go?"

"Of course." Even though my parents never attended church, they had no objections to my going.

I continued going to that little church long after the week of VBS ended and learned lots about Jesus. Life moved along like a lazy creek in summer.

"Good morning, sophomore class." The tall man smiled. "My name is Mr. Tim Black, and I'm your history teacher for this term."

Mr. Black was more than a teacher. He opened his home and heart to the students where he led a Bible study group. I became friends with his wife, Samantha, and often babysat their children.

"Here's something for you to read." Mr. Black held out a small booklet to me one day after class.

"Thank you."

I glanced at the title: *The Four Spiritual Laws.* Campus Crusade for Christ was sweeping through schools all over the country, and Mr. Black was actively involved in it.

"Just as there are physical laws that govern the physical universe, so are there spiritual laws that govern your relationship with God," I read in the booklet, later that day. "Law One ... God loves you."

Alone in my bedroom, I accepted and submitted to the endless love of God.

I maintained my friendship with Tim and Samantha Black, even after they moved to Alaska.

Come up and visit, Samantha wrote after I'd graduated high school. *You would love this church we're going to.*

I flew up and immediately latched onto the church, which was starting a new Bible school.

"I would really like to attend," I told Samantha. "I have no college plans at this point, so the timing is perfect."

"Sounds great. We'll talk to the pastor. Families are opening their homes to students, and he can assign you to one."

"That would be so perfect."

I moved in with Josh and Shelley Stewart. They hosted Pam, another girl, at the same time. They had small children, and we meshed into one diverse, happy, eclectic family together.

After three years, Tim and Samantha moved back to the Lower 48, settling in San Marcos, Texas, where he pastored a church.

"Josh and I have been talking," Shelley told me one day after Tim and Samantha had been gone for a year. "We are thinking of moving to San Marcos to help Tim with his church."

I looked at Pam. "What will we do?"

"I don't know," Pam said.

"You'll both come with us, of course," Shelley said. "We can't break up this crazy, happy family."

"Iowa to Alaska and now Texas." I shrugged. "Why not?"

We all moved, and I renewed my acquaintance with Tyson, a young man I'd met when I'd visited Tim and Samantha the previous year. We'd written some letters, as friends.

I attended a prayer meeting in Tim's home. *It's so good to be around Tim and Samantha again. And to see Tyson here.*

"Hi, Mia." Tyson's bright blue eyes twinkled. "You have any pressing plans for Saturday night?"

I smiled back at this wonderful young man, lately delivered from a life of drugs. He'd turned his life around, worked hard and studied the Bible with the thirst of a man lost on a Texas plain.

Tim grinned and nudged me. "Great catch," he whispered. Samantha nodded.

"Not that I know of," I told Tyson.

"Good. Then you'll have time to go to dinner with me."

My heart skipped like a stone across a pond when Tyson asked me to marry him a month later. I floated on a sea of contentment.

"God is giving you a good, solid Christian man," Shelley said. "You are so blessed."

Tyson worked hard, first as a furniture salesman and then in real estate. He put in long hours to keep me, and later our three children, in the best clothes, nicest cars and eventually a lovely, spacious home.

His work ethic provided an income that left me free to stay home as a full-time mother. Tyson handled all the bills and financial decisions. I reveled in God's amazing goodness of home, husband and family.

Our home buzzed with the voices of many young people who attended the Bible studies that Tyson led. I smiled inside and out as I provided fresh-baked cookies while they crowded around the dining table and fired questions at my husband.

When the economic downturn in the early 1980s put a strain on Tyson, he worked harder and longer hours. I missed his presence, but I knew he was doing it for his family.

"I just can't go this year," Tyson told me in October of 1985, as we discussed a trip to Iowa. "Airfare for five is just too expensive. I'll stay home."

"You work so hard, you need the break. Besides, who knows how long it will be before we can afford to all fly again?"

"We can't afford it now. I'll stay home."

"We can make it happen," I said. "It just won't be the same without you."

"Sorry, honey. Just can't do it this year. Maybe things will turn around for next year."

"See you when you get back." Tyson kissed me goodbye and then each of our three children, ages 3, 6 and 7. "Have fun at Grandma and Grandpa's."

We flew to Dallas where we'd catch a connecting flight to Iowa. Just as we landed, we smelled an awful odor, and some passengers spotted smoke coming from beneath the plane.

"This is your captain speaking. Please remain calm, and listen to the flight attendants' instructions. Emergency personnel are already waiting for us at the gate."

The attendants strode up and down the narrow aisle, speaking words of comfort in firm, calm tones.

"Please, miss," I said. "I have to get to my son and daughter. They're sitting up there." I pointed to seats several rows ahead of me.

"I will personally see to them," she promised. "Just remain seated, stay calm and follow instructions."

The moment the plane stopped, all exit doors were popped open.

"I have to get to my children!" I cried.

"Please stay calm," the attendant repeated. "I'll make sure they are safe." She moved through the passengers until she got to them. "I have them!"

We exited the plane, hearts pounding, confused and full of unanswered questions.

Clutching my youngest son in my arms, I grabbed my

other son and daughter and made my way through the airport. "Come on!" I exclaimed. "We have to make our next flight." We sprinted to the gate and settled into our seats just before the door closed.

Made it. I settled back to calm my nerves before seeing my parents. *I'll call Tyson from Mom's and let him know we are all okay. He'll be worried if he hears this on the news.*

We filed into the Iowa terminal where several black-suited men stopped me.

"We need to talk to you, ma'am," one intoned, flashing his I.D. "FBI."

"Why?"

"You were on the flight to Dallas?"

"Yes. Is this about the fire after we landed?"

"Please come with us," the other agent said. He led the four of us into a small room.

"What is this all about?" I asked.

"We traced an explosive to your luggage," an agent said.

"My luggage?" I squeaked. "You must be joking."

"We never joke," his partner said. "Especially about bombs."

I touched each boy's shoulder. "I have no knowledge about a bomb," I insisted. "I'm taking my children to see their grandparents. Why on earth would I want to bomb the plane out of the sky?"

After many hours, the FBI allowed my parents to drive us to their home, but they showed up the next day, with the press trailing. Mom's phone rang and rang with calls from reporters with endless questions.

My brother showed up the following day.

"Are you okay?" he almost shouted when he saw me sitting at Mom's table.

"Of course," I said. "Why wouldn't I be?"

"I was having coffee in town," he said. "Look at this article in the paper. *Your* name. They say you were involved in trying to blow up the plane."

"I don't understand," I said. "Why do they only show *my* name? I'm sure everyone on that flight must've been questioned."

A few days later we headed back home to Texas. *At last. I need Tyson's help in getting all this straightened out.*

"It's so good to see you," I said, throwing my arms around my strong, capable husband. "For some crazy reason, the FBI is pinning this bombing attempt on me. Do you believe it?"

"It'll all blow over soon enough. Let's just make life as normal as we can until it does."

Tyson continued working late every night. I felt sorry for him because I could read the stress in his face. The FBI was grilling him, too.

My heart burst with love and pride a few Sundays later as Tyson stood in front of our church.

"I want to thank everybody for your help and kindness at this time," he said. "It's been so hard on our family with all these false accusations. Thank you for your love and prayers."

Poor man. How can the FBI suspect my dear husband? He looks so tired. So stressed out.

One night, as usual, Tyson called. It was 10 p.m. "I'll be home within the hour," he promised.

The hour passed. No Tyson. Two hours passed. Then three.

I started to panic. *Whoever planted that bomb in my luggage must be trying to take him out. He must be hurt — or worse.*

When he still hadn't come home the next day, I called the police to file a Missing Person Report. Then I called my pastor's wife.

"Tyson's disappeared," I cried. "I'm so scared that something bad has happened to him. We could be next."

"Bring the kids and stay here for a few days," she said.

"I will. Thank you!"

The next three days were excruciating. "He's dead, I just know he's dead," I cried to God in the privacy of the guest bedroom. "They've killed him, and they're going to kill me next."

Mia! I felt a voice deep in my being. I believe it was God speaking to me. *You can either lay there and die, or you can get up. What is it going to be?*

I crawled to my knees, placed my hands on the bedpost and pulled myself to my feet.

"I have to get up. For the children, I have to get up."

The FBI came to my pastor's house for more questioning. "I want you to know that I know he did this," I said as soon as we all sat down.

Surprise arched their collective eyebrows north.

"Yes." I laid two receipts in front of them. "I found these in our bedroom the other day."

The men studied them. One, from American Express, showed the charges for our flight to Iowa. The other showed that he'd purchased extra insurance in the unlikely event that we all perished in a plane crash. He stood to collect more than 2 million dollars. But the whole flight had to die for him to collect.

"Takes a load off our minds." The agent allowed himself a ghost of a smile. "We thought we were going to have to convince you about this. Your husband is our *only* suspect."

"You reported him missing," the other said.

"Yes."

"You have any idea where he might go?"

"Las Vegas. I'm sure he thinks he can lose himself there." I cleared my throat. "I've already canceled the credit cards."

"Good thing. We have an APB (All Points Bulletin) out on him. It's going to be on the news, so you need to be prepared. You'll let us know if you hear from him?"

"Of course."

A few days later, the FBI arrested Tyson at the Las Vegas airport when he tried to buy a ticket on a canceled credit card.

I took my kids home and began learning the depth of Tyson's deception. He'd been spending huge sums of money on cocaine, was stealing from work and had stopped paying our mortgage. I lost the house, the cars, everything. And I had to explain his absence to three confused, young children.

"When's Daddy coming home?"

"He's not, honey. Daddy will be away for a very long time."

"Why not?"

"Well, Daddy did something very bad, and now he has to pay for that."

"How?"

"You know how when we go to McDonald's, I have to pay for your Happy Meals with money?"

"Yes."

"I have to pay before you can eat, right?"

"Yes."

"Well, Daddy has to pay for what he's done before he can come back home."

"What's Daddy done?"

"I'm sorry, but you have to wait until you're a little older for me to explain. For now, just trust Mommy that you are all safe and someday Daddy will be allowed to come home again."

I moved the children into a duplex and started my own drapery business. Then, as I like to think of it, God "showed up to show off."

"Would you like some beef?" one friend asked. "We just butchered a cow and need the freezer space."

God constantly stretched food for us. One chicken could feed our family of four for three days. My son's class "adopted us" and showered us with food and presents for Christmas.

Even with mounting evidence against him, I continued believing in Tyson. *He'll get off the drugs. He'll turn his life around like he did before. When he gets out of jail, we can go back to being a family again.*

I took the children to visit their father in jail, where, for a few hours, the justice system allowed us to be a family again.

A year passed. The FBI came to see me again.

"We're going for two consecutive sentences of 20 years each," an agent informed me.

"Forty years?" My voice climbed an octave. "What am I supposed to do for 40 years? Isn't this overkill?"

"Look, lady." Another agent leaned close and locked eyes with me. "I've dealt with lots of criminals in my time. People get caught up in things and do stuff they regret later." He rested his weight on his knuckles. "I've seen lots of guys sorry for what they've done later." He paused. "I don't see that here. This guy has no regrets, nor does he love you."

I stayed up late that night to talk to God. A week before, I'd had a bad dream. In it, I saw my husband sneak up and kill me from behind while I watched from a distance. Anger rose up in me. *How could you do this?* I screamed in the dream. *How could you so nonchalantly plan to kill your wife and kids ... and others ... to get your butt out of trouble?*

The FBI agent only confirmed what the dream had tried to tell me. Even so, I fell on my knees and sobbed against the bed.

Mia, you are crying for all the wrong reasons, God said, deep in my heart. *You are crying for the judgment Tyson will get at sentencing.*

"That's true," I cried.

You should be crying for the state of his heart.

I sagged against the bed and felt, for the first time, a separating between Tyson and myself. *I need to divorce him.*

Yes. God read my thoughts. His incomprehensible, incomparable peace settled over me.

I sought counseling to deal with the shock, betrayal and lies and, through it, decided to let go of bitterness and forgive Tyson.

I'm writing to tell you that even though I am seeking a divorce, I forgive you for what you tried to do to us.

Why do you want to divorce? Tyson wrote back. *How did I hurt you?*

He doesn't know he hurt us? I stared at the paper. *He tried to kill 150 people, including his own wife and children who trusted him completely, and he can't see how he hurt us?*

My pastor's wife approached me two years after Tyson's thwarted attempt to advance his family into eternity.

"Would you like to share your testimony at the end of the Ladies Seminar coming up?"

I paused for a few moments. "Yes," I decided. "I want to thank everyone for their kindness to me in the wake of what happened. And, I don't know how he did it, but Tyson managed to deceive all of us. They need to know what I now know."

The night came. I stood and gazed over the loving faces of my many friends. I took a deep breath and began my story.

"Back in 1985, we began planning for the children and me to go to Iowa because we didn't know when we'd be able to afford it again, and I hadn't been home in more than two years. I had no idea, but Tyson was a cocaine addict. He used the drug every day, and it cost a lot, so he was wheeling, dealing and stealing to get cash to buy it.

"He began to feel like his life was so bad that he was too bad for us and that maybe he should take his own life. But that idea didn't appeal to him, so it became logical to him to take ours instead. While driving in his car one day and listening to a talk show, he learned about a crime that had taken place when somebody had bought a bomb through an ad in the *Soldier of Fortune* magazine. He bought the magazine and ordered the bomb, supposedly to put it on a small airplane to blow up. This is what he told the person he bought the bomb from.

"He kept the bomb in his desk at work for more than a month. It probably would've done the job, but he wanted to add more gunpowder because it was going on a much larger plane. So, he took it apart and broke the clock, which, in the end, saved our lives. The night before we left, he bought three different clocks, trying to get the right size, but couldn't find one small enough.

"He took the clothes out of one bag and put the bomb inside. Then he drove us to the airport, kissed us all goodbye and sent us off to die. Dollar signs were probably rolling around in his head because he stood to collect 2.6 million dollars in insurance — more than twice as much as was first reported — and he thought that this would solve his problems."

I fell silent for a few moments. "God protects his children," I continued, "because the bomb went off at the one and only possible safe place. We'd just landed in Dallas and were taxiing toward the gates when we felt the pop. We all knew something was wrong. The tower directed us to the first available gate, and workers jumped into action, unloading the gasoline and baggage and passengers.

"When they opened the pod, the bomb went off, and flames shot up in the air. The terrible smells of something burning and jet fuel terrified us all.

"But through this event, God has shown his love and protection, even when we don't know we need it.

"The bomb was supposed to explode during the flight, but I've been told American Airlines is the only one which stores baggage in pods. The pod kept the bomb contained, and lack of air kept it from detonating until we were on the ground. And nobody, not even the handlers, was hurt.

"So, as shocked as we all are and have been, we have to acknowledge that God truly does watch over us and keeps us safe, even when we have no clue of our impending danger."

"Mia, can you share how God got you through this hard time?"

"With pleasure. I asked God — well, actually, I asked God many questions — but, one particular time, I asked him how a Christian could get to the point of committing such a heinous sin. God told me, *With one little compromise at a time.* Then he showed me James 1:12: 'Blessed is the man who perseveres under trial, because when he has stood the test, he will receive the crown of life that God has promised to those who love him.' I knew this was a test, but God showed he is always with me, even in the darkest times.

"I then asked God how a Christian overcomes temptation, and he told me, *One obedience at a time*, and then he showed me Romans 6:16: 'Obedience leads to righteousness.'"

"How about your children?" another asked. "You must've been terribly worried about how this would affect them."

"Of course! But God gave me another verse, Isaiah

54:13: 'Great will be your children's peace.' I hung onto that one phrase through all the confusion and pain and fear. God himself promised to give my children peace — and he has."

"What was the greatest thing you learned?"

"God showed me that I used to be a 'giver-upper' all my life, but facing this tragedy with Tyson made me into a 'goer on-er.' I didn't just survive the deception, I *overcame*."

I took a long, hard look in the mirror in 1988. "You know what, Mia?" I allowed myself a slight smile. "I'm not looking for a husband, but should someone ask me out, I'm going to say yes."

"Hi, Mia." My friend Marcia called soon after. "How're you doing?"

"I'd be fine except my kids have been down with chicken pox for six weeks. I'm going stir crazy!"

"Your birthday is coming up, right?"

"Yes, soon."

"I know this really fantastic guy. He works with my husband and was widowed earlier this year. Would you let him take you out for your birthday?"

Unbeknownst to me, she'd already called and asked John if he'd take her friend — me — out, and his response was, "I'm the man for the job."

"Well, sure," I answered. *What could it hurt?*

A few days later, the doorbell rang. A delivery man stood on my porch, holding a long, narrow box.

"Mrs. Johnson?"

"Yes."

"These are for you."

I gasped. He held out a huge bouquet of beautiful roses.

Later, the phone rang.

"Hello, Mia? John here."

"Oh, thank you for the lovely roses!"

"I'm sorry they're so impersonal, but I didn't know what to get you."

"Impersonal! They're perfect."

"I understand Marcia is going to meet us at the restaurant (he named a place halfway between our two homes) and introduce us."

"That will be fun. I'm looking forward to it."

Marcia decided to bring another mutual friend, Jessica, for my first meeting with John.

"God," I prayed on the long drive, "I don't want to be fooled again. Please show me this man's heart."

"Mia!" Marcia stood and waved from a restaurant booth. "Over here."

I walked over.

"This is John. John, Mia."

The ladies beamed and chattered and lingered. Finally, John stood up.

"Ladies, may I show you to your cars?"

They laughed — and left.

John and I laughed, too, from nervous jitters. But we sat and talked — and talked. Hours passed like moments as we shared our lives.

"Maybe we'd better go before the restaurant makes us wash dishes," I said.

"Don't want that," John agreed, "but before we do, can we pray together?"

This is his true heart, I felt God saying. I wiped away tears. I knew I would marry this man and that God had orchestrated this meeting.

"John." I phoned him a few days later.

"Hello, Mia. I was just thinking about you."

"We have a little problem."

"What is that?"

"Well, you see, my church is a bit protective of me because they witnessed the pain and confusion I went through because of Tyson."

"And?"

"They sorta want to interview you." I swallowed. "Sorry."

John's warm laugh reached through the wires and embraced me. "Not a problem. I'll set up an appointment. If they didn't grill me, then I wouldn't know they care about you so much."

Of course, John passed what we like to call the Gentle Inquisition without a hitch, which opened the door for us to get hitched soon thereafter.

I began attending John's church after our wedding, and in 2003, the pastor announced plans to start a new church in Leander.

"I think we should be part of the group that goes," John said.

"I agree. How exciting to help a church get started and be part of the process from day one."

The new church, Believers Church in Leander, continued the tradition of solid teaching, vibrant worship and genuine friendships.

"Thank you for your service." John grins up at our server in our favorite restaurant and holds out a card with his picture on it. "We'd like to invite you to come to Believers Church. You'll be family the moment you walk through the door!"

She takes the card.

"You'll find the directions and times we meet on the other side. You'll be a part of wonderful, real worship and hear good teaching from Pastor RJ. We look forward to seeing you there!"

Dare to Dream Again

The Story of Araya

Written by Melissa Harding

I sat on the bed trying to make sense of what was going on. The heavy smell of smoke that always lingered in our home crept up my nose as fear circled my heart. Tears spilled down my mom's cheeks as she tried to explain her decision.

"I'm leaving Dad, Araya. I can't live here anymore," she choked out, grabbing my trembling hands.

"Why, Mommy?" I asked. My 4-year-old mind couldn't understand what this meant. "Please don't go."

"It'll be okay, sweetie. I promise." She sniffed, wiping away her tears. "I'm going to live with Grandpa. You can't come with me. He doesn't want kids in his house, but someday soon I'll come back for you. I'll always be your mom."

The brown suitcase rolled noisily down the driveway, scraping its rusty wheels on the uneven concrete, my mom's determined grip guiding it down the path to her car. Away from the nightmare of our home. Away from the senseless beatings and drunken brawls.

She'll be back, I thought as I watched the car until it faded into a tiny red dot on the horizon.

The Road Leads Home

I gulped for air, but saltwater filled my lungs. The seaweed was tangled around me, forming an inescapable prison. My weak arms tried to swim against the current, but it was too strong. My brother Alex and I were playing in the ocean, unaware of its deadly power. No one was watching our 5- and 6-year-old bodies to make sure we came back up after each pounding swell. No one would see the jaws of this foaming monster swallow me whole. Mustering a strength found only in the depths of desperation, Alex broke the seaweed chains, and together we crawled across the wet sand, our lungs burning with every gasp. We ran home, desperate for the safety of our father's arms. Desperate to know someone would take care of us. And there we found him, passed out cold on the floor.

"Here, get his other arm, and we'll drag him to bed," my brother said, taking one of my dad's arms while I grabbed the other. We dragged his limp body across the filthy floor, trying not to trip over the clothes and trash strewn throughout the house.

Alex and I took care of ourselves the best we knew how. We lived in a small city in Southern California, in a rough neighborhood and even rougher home. There was never enough food, and my stomach always cried out for more. We played basketball in our driveway late into the night, surrounded by gangs and danger, while our dad drowned his sorrows in bottle after bottle of beer. Most nights, he passed out before we came in, and we put him to bed and locked up the house without a second thought.

On other nights, Dad took us with him to the houses of various women he knew. We played in the living room, waiting for him to emerge from a back room and take us home.

Shadows crept across the wall, my heart racing against the clock. But on nights like these, my heart always won the race. A clock was no competition for a little heart frantic with fear. Tucked beneath the covers next to my dad, I could smell the alcohol emanating from his breath and clothes. The bitter taste of dread rose again to my mouth, and I waited for the inevitable. The three of us slept in the same bed. I was too scared to sleep alone, and I wanted to be close to my dad, to know there was someone still here to protect me. But my dad did things in his drunken stupor — things no one dared speak about in the light of day. In the wee hours of the night, the hands that should have shielded me from the horrors of this world instead became the hands that wandered, the hands I dreaded. I just wanted to make him happy. I wanted to please him. I wanted to please everyone, but I always fell short.

This must be punishment for not being good enough. Maybe if I just try harder, I can make him happy.

I learned how to hide my fear. I learned how to block the pain. I learned how to hide inside myself instead of facing the truth.

The Road Leads Home

The knife grazed my skin, warning me not to move another inch. My heart stopped as I looked into the menacing eyes of my cousin. *How could this be happening?* My aunt lived close by, so on days I was sick, she would take care of me. She wasn't always there, though. And on those days, my cousin made it clear who was in charge.

His words slithered down my spine, and I could feel his breath on my face.

"I'm going to touch you, and I'm going to tell you to do things to me that you aren't going to tell anyone. If you do, I will kill you."

The knife against my throat was all he needed to convince me he meant what he said. So I obeyed. I always obeyed. It was part of me, this deep desire to please and obey. And yet I never could do things right. It was all my fault. I couldn't ignore the nagging feeling that there must be something in me to cause people to do this.

I'm just not good enough.

The kids made fun of me at school for the way I looked and the way I dressed. We didn't have any clean clothes, and I often wore my brother's old clothes to school. My little body practically disappeared in the baggy clothes, and I wished I could just disappear altogether.

Even in kindergarten, I walked myself to and from school. Many days I went to the park instead of school to avoid the taunting and ridicule. I didn't want to face anyone or anything, so I lived in my own world — a world where Daddy didn't drink and Mommy stayed to take care of me.

Screams filled the house. The argument in the living room escalated, the voices thundering with rage as my mom and dad fought over our custody. I didn't know which I feared more: the explosion of angry shouting all around me, the possibility Dad would take us away or my conflicting allegiances. My mom had taken us to live with her and her new husband. Everything was ready and waiting for us. A new world, full of freedom and hope, beckoned my aching heart. They didn't think Dad would find us, but he did. Not even a day had passed before he arrived, pounding on the door, heaving in fury. My hope evaporated in the blaze of their hatred.

"You're the one who abandoned them, Lily! I've been taking care of them for years, and now you think you can just waltz in and take them from me?" Dad yelled, his face flushed with both anger and beer.

"Fine," she conceded, "let them decide. Kids, who do you want to live with? Me or Dad?"

I sat on the bed, looking around at the new clothes and toys spilling across the room. *This should be an easy decision,* I thought. But I loved my dad. I didn't want to make him angry. I wanted to obey and make him proud of me. The thought of disappointing him ate at my heart.

Was the freedom this new life promised worth the sacrifice of letting my dad down?

I looked over at Alex. "Well, what do you want to do?"

"Are you crazy, Araya! We're not going back to that hell hole! We're staying here!"

My dad came in the room, looking like a lost puppy. His eyes searched for mine, as I hung my head in shame.

"So, what do you want to do?"

"Dad, I love you," I whispered.

"Do you want to come live with me?" he demanded.

"I love you, but I'm going to stay here with Mom." I was 7. My voice squeaked out the words I knew would break his heart.

Years passed before I saw my dad again. He didn't show up for his weekends with us. I was certain I was being punished for my disobedience and that I deserved it. All I ever wanted was to make my dad happy, and I just couldn't do it. Anger swelled like the ocean tide within me. But as much as I tried to blame him, I couldn't hide anymore from the ugly truth I saw when I looked in the mirror. I was disgusted with myself and the things I had done. I didn't deserve a happy life. I didn't deserve to be loved.

There must be something wrong with me, I concluded.

The wind blew back my hair, and a giggle burst from my mouth. I gazed up at the twinkling stars, their lights dancing as if winking at me. As if they knew a naughty secret I was about to discover.

Jesse, my best friend, convinced me to ride our bikes to a party at the beach. It was my first sleepover with someone other than my extended family. *If my parents found out we'd left Jesse's house, they'd kill me,* I thought. But they wouldn't find out. We were just going for a little while to have some fun.

When we arrived, a group of high-schoolers were gathered around a fire pit, drinking and laughing. The bonfire cracked and spit flames all around us, and my strawberry-flavored drink tickled my taste buds. It slid down my throat like water over glass. One more wouldn't hurt, right? Besides, it felt so good just to forget everything and have fun for once. But once I started, I couldn't stop. I drank and drank and drank.

I was 13, and I was drunk.

We stumbled over our bikes, trying to make them go in the direction of Jesse's home.

"What on earth are you girls doing out here?"

Oh no, I thought, panicking. *I know that voice. Maybe I can just pretend like I'm fine and she won't notice anything different.*

When we didn't come home as expected from our bike ride, Jesse's parents called mine, and then all our parents came looking for us.

"We … were … just … getting some fresh air," I lied, trying to remember how to bring words from my brain down into my mouth. The earth was spinning, and my thoughts jumbled over each other, like a jigsaw puzzle that had been dropped on the floor.

"You think I don't know what someone looks like when she's drunk, Araya?" my mom asked, disgust dripping from her voice.

I could see the disappointment on her face, and shame welled up within me like an iron weight, forever pinning me to the past.

This was only the beginning of my love affair with alcohol. At first, I just wanted to have fun and do what everyone else seemed to be doing. My grandparents drank, my dad drank and my stepdad drank. Every family gathering involved alcohol. It couldn't be that bad, right? Soon, I craved its sweet taste and gentle embrace. It made me fearless. I could sit on the roof of a car and drive through town without a care in the world. I was invincible. I was free.

The years went by, and no matter how hard I wanted to be a good girl, I grew tired of feeling like I was never good enough. So I drank. And I lied. And when I got caught, my parents' anger hung like smoke in our home. They were disgusted with me, and nothing I did made it better. Memories clouded my vision as bitterness ate away at anything good in my life.

What kind of mother leaves her children to be abused by their father? If she hadn't left us, my heart would still be whole. How can a mother leave her child?

What kind of father takes advantage of his innocent daughter?

I couldn't escape my thoughts. They were incessant reminders. They followed me everywhere. The pain was too much, so many nights I drank myself into oblivion.

There was something about churches that I always recognized as special. When I was little, I used to walk myself to a Catholic church near our home. Like the park, it was a place I felt safe. I liked hearing about God, but I didn't really feel I deserved to be loved. I had done too many things wrong to be forgiven. God wasn't someone I could know. And even if I could, I figured he probably wouldn't want to know me. The void inside me grew bigger, and I wanted more. I wanted something that could fill the gaping holes in my heart.

I started dating Josh at 18, and he swept me into a new world of hope and love. During the months that followed, I grew hungry to know more about God. I accompanied him to services at his non-denominational church, and I fell in love with the people. They talked about God as if they actually knew him. They worshipped him as if they were actually speaking to him.

Josh's mom took me under her wing and told me about Jesus and how he died on the cross for me, to pay for all the things I'd done wrong. She told me how the God who created this world also created me perfectly, just the way I am. I saw the love of God in her love for me, and for the first time in my life, I believed that I was worth something. Like a sponge, my dry heart soaked up her words, and a newfound joy dazzled before me.

On New Year's Eve, as one year faded into the next, I realized how much I longed for peace. I craved the hope and freedom from my shame promised in Jesus. While fireworks lit up the darkness, their incandescent rainbows sizzling into the night sky, my heart accepted the forgiveness of God. Light and peace flooded my heart as tears spilled down my face. An inexplicable joy overwhelmed me, and I knew I had finally found where I belonged.

My joy was short-lived as reality returned, seizing me up in its chaos. My friends didn't like the new Araya. They quickly grew tired of my excitement and fervor for God.

"Why can't you just be the same girl you were before?" they beckoned.

Without enough self-esteem to hold my ground, I dove right back into the world I knew before. And I fell hard.

"I thought I told you not to wear that dress, Araya," Adam hissed in my ear, squeezing my wrist so tightly, my fingers turned white. "Why can't you just do what I tell you to do? Why are you so stupid?"

"Please stop, you're hurting me," I whispered, looking around at the people walking past, wondering if anyone could see the pain in my eyes. It never occurred to me to find help. This was normal. I wouldn't get anything better than this, so I decided to just make the best of it.

"Believe me, I could hurt you a lot worse than this if I wanted to. Just shut up, and do what I say."

Later that day, mustering the thread of dignity I still held, I told him I couldn't take it anymore.

"I'm tired of this, Adam. You can't treat me like this anymore." As I spoke up for myself, I gulped in a breath of relief and braced myself for his response.

Fury rushing to his face, Adam charged toward me and pushed me hard against the wall.

"If you leave me, I'm going to kill you," he threatened, each word stinging like a slap across the face.

He punched me in the stomach and threw me on the tile floor. I hit the tile, and pain seared through my face. I realized there was no point trying to leave. I was powerless against him, and he knew it.

Adam knelt beside me. He brushed the hair away from my face, trailing his fingers across the bruise growing on my cheek, and said, "No one else can have you, Araya. You are mine."

I surrendered to his control. After all, I didn't deserve better than this. God didn't have anything better for me, so why fight it? Months passed. My only solace was the fact that I hadn't given myself to Adam sexually. I wanted to wait until I got married.

"Come on, baby, you know that I love you. Stop fighting this."

The afternoon was hot, but the heat between us

burned with rising passion. We had the house to ourselves, and one thing quickly led to another.

"No, we have to stop," I begged, praying he wouldn't get angry and lash out again.

Without a word, he forced me into his sister's bedroom and held me down.

"No! Stop!" I struggled against his weight, trying to wrestle out from under him. "No ..." I whimpered before letting my body fall limp with surrender. "I hate you."

It didn't matter. My feeble attempts to resist him were pointless. He had his way with me, and I had no choice but to concede. Once again, my thoughts assailed me, digging the shame deeper into my soul.

This is the way it's supposed to be. This is the best I'm going to get. I'm never going to get away from this. After all, I deserve it.

My family knew I was in trouble, but I turned a blind eye to the truth. My brother Danny saw beyond my fake smile and refused to accept Adam. One day, Adam followed Danny and me home, taunting me with threats and accusations. I gripped Danny's hand, and we ran for our lives. After nearly two years of denial, the scales on my eyes finally fell away. When I saw my own fear reflected in my little brother's eyes, I knew something had to change. Even if I didn't think I deserved to be protected, I would do whatever it took to protect my family. We moved away, safe from Adam's threats and demands. But while I may have been safe, I was far from free.

From the outside, with his dashing smile and regal Navy uniform, Derek exuded confidence, romance and security. He smooth-talked his way into my heart, impressing me with both his exemplary values and knowledge of the Bible. The façade faded as the real man lurking beneath the glossy veneer of a gentleman leaked through. His words sliced me apart, but I couldn't resist his manipulative charm. I turned a blind eye to his patterns of self-pity, distracted by the endless parties and incessant drinking. Like a dog returns to its vomit, I returned again and again to his verbal berating.

"You don't need me," Derek whined again, stoking the embers of inadequacy within me. Oh, but I did need him, and he knew it. Even after breaking off our engagement, I ran back to him when I realized how lost he was without me. After desperately trying for years to make the people in my life happy, here was a man I could help. Finally, someone needed me. I could save him. Maybe I was never good enough for my dad or Adam, but Derek needed me. I would be enough for him. I could rescue him. And so, pushing aside any prickling doubts, we got married.

We moved to Florida, a new beginning beckoning me with the luster of promise. But life carried on the same as it had before.

The Road Leads Home

My hands trembled as I pushed back the curtain of the picture-frame window in our living room.

Our baby boy, Matthew, slept soundly in the room down the hall. My suspicions of Derek's unfaithfulness couldn't be ignored any longer. He burst through the door and looked over at me, a shadow covering his eyes. I squared my shoulders, hoping I looked more confident than I felt.

"Are you having an affair, Derek?" No use beating around the bush. I had to get it out before I lost my nerve.

"What? How dare you ask me something like that. You don't have any proof. And besides, it's none of your business what I do with my time," he answered, the blood rising in his cheeks as the rage rose in his voice.

"I have a right to know. I'm your wife, and I deserve to know if you're cheating on me."

I closed my eyes and heard the slap across my cheek. The more I fought back, the more violent he became, pushing me down and punching me again and again.

I'm not going to live through this. The room spun around me. *I'm not pretty enough for him. I'm not a good enough wife. I'm just not enough.*

He was my husband, and divorce wasn't the answer. I just needed to try harder.

"I'm gonna leave you. I'm done with this marriage!" Derek yelled, grabbing his golf club and stomping toward the door.

"NO, I want to talk about it!" I grabbed the golf club, trying to keep him from leaving.

"Why are you always in my business?" He threw the golf club across the room and leapt for my throat.

Rough hands clenched my neck, constricting the air like a kink in a hose. Fighting with every ounce of strength I possessed, I thrashed against him, escaping long enough to gasp for air and pry open the window.

Derek stormed out the door, bellowing his disappointment with me and our marriage.

"Oh, God, please fix my marriage!" I cried out, collapsing into a heap on the kitchen floor. In my hopelessness, I turned once again to my faithful friend, alcohol. Desperate to numb the pain, I drank until I couldn't feel anymore.

The next morning, guilt replaced the pain with hollow regret. How did I end up in this place? With my baby sleeping down the hall, what could have happened to him while I was drunk? How can I raise him in this madness? Even if I didn't deserve better than this, I wanted to give my son a chance. He deserved a happy childhood. But I couldn't give up on my marriage. I kept holding on, hoping and praying that things would change. I could fix this. Somehow, I would figure out a way to make him want me again — to make him want to stay.

The fighting increased with Derek's unfaithfulness. My work at the YMCA consumed me. I wasn't drinking as much now that I had Matthew, but I still needed something to help with the pain. So I threw myself into my work, masking my sorrow with professional success. It felt good to do something right and be rewarded for it.

On Thanksgiving, our little family gathered around a table laden with the food I had spent all day preparing.

Derek looked into my eyes and said flatly, "That's it. I'm leaving you for good."

Derek wasn't coming back. It was over. Depression settled over me like a cloud that never left. Its heaviness followed me like a shadow, a constant reminder of my failures and inadequacies.

I didn't want to wake up and face this nightmare all over again. I didn't want to live. The pitter-patter of little feet down the hall reminded me why I needed to get up.

Matthew. Oh, my sweet little boy. I would get out of bed for him. I would put one foot in front of the other and somehow make it through another day for him.

My hand flew instinctively to my belly. I ran my fingers over my swollen midsection, remembering the life growing inside.

Derek's baby. Oh, God, how can I be a single mother to two children?

Fear slithered up into my mind, drawing me back into the murky well of despair. I couldn't crawl my way out of this hopelessness. How would I get through this?

I had stopped going to church — turned my back on God. My life was such a mess, and I knew I wasn't worthy to be in his presence. Anger welled up within me. Where was God in all of this? If he really was so good and loving, then why was I here alone, trying to pick up the pieces of my shattered life?

Just when I thought I couldn't sink any deeper, my little brother called with news of a job at a YMCA in Texas, close to where he and my mom and stepdad lived.

"Araya, this would be perfect for you. Come on, you gotta at least apply," he coaxed again and again.

"I don't know, Danny. I'm probably not qualified, and I can't afford to move across the country."

"Oh, come on. Just try! You'll never know if you don't at least give it a shot," he said.

That night, I got on my knees and asked God what he wanted me to do. I didn't know what would happen, but I knew I couldn't continue on the path I was on. My kids deserved a chance.

As I prayed, I realized how, little by little, bitterness had taken over my life. It seeped through my veins, like a poison, infecting every part of me. I had to let it go. I had to stop blaming God for everything that had happened to me. I wanted hope. I wanted life. I wanted more than the endless days of agony, pining over my lost marriage.

"God, forgive me for turning my back on you! I'm so afraid to raise these kids by myself, but I can't do it alone anymore. I need you to show me what to do!" I begged, sobs racking through my body.

My child, it's time to move on. It's time to let it go, came a gentle whisper, and peace engulfed my soul. I felt God's presence wash over me, and I knew I wasn't alone. I could face the future with him. I could forgive the people who had hurt me and see them through new eyes. My vision cleared as I looked back on my life and the little girl who just wanted to make everyone happy. My whole life I had been trying to be good enough, but I always fell short. I didn't have to try to fix things anymore. When God looked at me, I realized, he didn't see my failures or shortcomings. He saw me as beautiful. He saw me as pure because of Jesus' sacrifice on my behalf. My fear fled as I rose with newfound hope and direction.

By what could only be a miracle, I was offered the job. With all expenses paid for, I moved back to Texas with the joy and freedom that came from knowing God would never leave me, and I could rest in his unfailing arms.

It took time to embrace the fullness of my freedom in Christ. My dependency on alcohol worsened over the years. At first, I permitted myself an occasional fun night with my friends while the kids spent summers with Derek. Eventually, my drinking raged out of control. Even though I knew God loved me and had good plans for my life, I still couldn't escape the pain of the past. The only thing I knew to do was simply lose myself in the empty promises of another drink.

After one night of intense drinking, I realized if something didn't stop, I would turn into my father. I thought about my sweet boys at home, depending on me to take care of them. I didn't deserve their trust, but they offered it to me with arms open wide. I decided it was time to change, and I knew I couldn't do it on my own.

After years of thinking I couldn't go to church until I cleaned up my life, I finally conceded to my brother's pleas to go regardless of my excuses. I found a church that believed in the power of prayer.

When doctors found a lump in my breast, I went forward one Sunday, asking God to show up in a real way. People surrounded me, and I felt overwhelmed with love. As they prayed, a sensation swept over me, and heat radiated across my chest. I wept with joy because I knew that something had changed in my body.

When I returned to the doctors, they couldn't find a trace of anything. I couldn't believe that God loved me so much, he would do something like this for me. I realized that if God could heal my body, then maybe he could heal my heart as well.

With my eyes set on Jesus, I walked day by day in his love, relying on his strength to heal my pain. He was faithful, and I am free!

The knocking at the door echoed the pounding in my heart. It felt as if it was beating outside of my chest, thumping in my ears. Today was the day I would meet Peter. He and I had been communicating through e-mails for two months, and we were finally going out on a real date. I smoothed out my dress, walked to the door and turned the handle, hoping he wouldn't notice my shaking hands.

This is the man you're going to marry, came the gentle whisper I had grown to know so well. I was about to go on a date with a man I didn't know, and this unexpected news jolted my confidence.

"What? God, I just met the man. Did you have to tell me this now?" I asked, trying to regain my composure in the bathroom.

Was I even ready for this? How could I trust someone after all that had happened in my life? Every man I ever loved had taken my heart and wrung it out like a wet rag. Would it be any different this time?

I fought against the negative thoughts and planted my feet on the truth of my new identity in Christ. Although I was never promised an easy road, I knew that God had good things in store for me. He had dreams for my life that I had never even imagined. I could run and hide from those dreams, or I could simply trust that he had my life in his hands.

The day I met Peter, I knew my life would never be the same. When he came to the door for our first date, I knew there was something special about this man. As time went by, I realized that this was a man worth waiting for. Peter didn't just talk about God, he breathed God's love with his life. He proposed on the beach, and we were married five months later. Despite my fears that it was too good to be true, Peter loved me with an unconditional love I had never known.

Dare to Dream Again

We moved to Leander, Texas, and joined Believers Church. The people here love us beyond anything we can comprehend. They've loved us through miscarriages and Crohn's disease. They've prayed with us, cried with us and laughed with us. I don't have to be perfect here. I can just be me, with all my baggage and history, and they love me, anyway.

The sun shimmers over the water, golden beams of light dancing across the horizon. The waves pound against the sand, and I breathe in the beauty all around me.

With each ebb and flow of the tide, I remember God's faithfulness through the joys and sorrows of life. Over the years, I've faced loss, sickness and death of loved ones. I know the sting of shattered dreams. I've felt the anguish of broken promises. Yet, even in my darkest hour, when life doesn't make sense and I cry out for answers, my hope remains steadfast.

I stare out at the sea, overwhelmed by the grandeur of its brilliance. The serenade of the waves sweeps me off my feet with a melody sweet and constant. The seagulls soar above me, joining in the chorus. I am loved beyond measure by the same God who created such a palette of wonder. He is bigger than any heartache, sickness or regret. He is bigger than the mistakes of my parents and the agony of my failures. I close my eyes, filling my lungs with the salty air, and hope surges within me.

I was once a broken little girl, wandering through the pieces of my fractured dreams. But now, as I spread out my arms and join in the song of creation, I dance because I'm free. The chains of the past don't hold me anymore. I'm free to soar. I'm free to dream again.

An Untrusting Heart
The Story of Emma
Written by Diana Leagh Matthews

This was a living nightmare.

"How can this be?" I asked Mom in disbelief. I stared out the kitchen window, focusing on nothing more than the sunlight. I needed to focus on something brighter than the dark place I was sinking into.

Dad was a hothead with a temper, but it seemed unfathomable that he had murdered his own brother in cold blood.

"There has to be a mistake," I said, shaking my head, but I could not get my mind around what I was hearing. This wasn't possible. I wanted to wake up and find this was nothing more than a terrible dream.

"I wish it were a mistake, but it's not," Mom assured me. She was just as heartbroken as I was.

"How could this happen?" I muttered through my tears as I stared into space.

By the time I was 5 years old, my parents had divorced. After seven years of marriage, Mom could no longer tolerate living with Dad.

My little brother and I would visit Dad on the cattle

farm, where he lived and worked, several times a year — Christmas, Spring Break and half of our summer vacation.

Dad's house was very small and cramped. The small covered cement front porch was flanked by the white horizontal paneling that wrapped the sides of the house. Inside there were two main bedrooms and one bathroom that we all shared. Dad closed in the back porch and made it into a bedroom for Derrick, my younger brother.

Dad was very untrusting. We never had privacy when using the phone in his house. Whenever we talked with Mom, he always listened in on the other line. I often heard Dad arguing with Mom over the phone about child support and other issues concerning Derrick and me.

Dad ran a cattle ranch with hundreds of cows. He would buy and sell the cattle and give them their immunizations. When we were young, Derrick and I didn't have any chores or responsibilities on the farm. But as we got older, Dad would try and get us to help out with the business.

Derrick and I would sit on the big iron gate and watch Dad run the cows through chutes, give them medication and brand them with a hot iron. We'd watch as the bull cows lost their tempers and charged at anything in their way. Smells of dirt, cow patties, hay bales and pine trees wafted up to us from the pastures near the house.

One rainy night, Dad had to deliver a calf. We brought the new calf into a pen near the house and named him Stormy. Derrick and I had so much fun feeding him with an oversized milk bottle.

I always appreciated that Dad encouraged Derrick and me to do really well in school and to study hard. To Dad, image was always top priority, so he continually checked to make sure our ears were clean, our hair was combed and our clothes showed no wrinkles. If we weren't doing what suited him, we'd trigger his temper.

When we were with Dad, Derrick and I spent a lot of our time with our grandmother, who lived next door in a beautiful old ranch house. As soon as Dad's white Dodge truck pulled out of the driveway, we would run over to Grandmother's house and enjoy the cheese eggs and homemade biscuits she made for us. We played hide-and-seek and cowboys and Indians in her well-manicured bushes and used the huge oak trees in her yard for bases when we played baseball.

When the hot Texas sun beat down, making life outside miserable, we enjoyed helping Grandmother with various activities inside the house. We loved spending time with her.

For a while, Uncle Thomas lived with Grandmother. He had soft white hair and a bald spot on the top of his head. He was always fun to be around, constantly had a smile on his face and made us feel loved.

"Let's box," he'd say, holding up his knuckled fists. We folded our hands and pretended to box with him. When we finished, we all laughed, and he pulled us into his large embrace, wrapping his arms around us in a fierce hug. He was very affectionate and always had the kindest look in his eyes.

"I'm going to get you!" He laughed, turning his hug into a tickling match. He loved to tickle us, but we didn't care. We knew he and Grandmother loved us, and we loved them in return. Sadly, we did not feel the same affection with our father.

Uncle Thomas and Dad did not get along. The two brothers often argued over various bills and other issues. Dad did not like Uncle Thomas living on the ranch with Grandmother. He was sure Uncle Thomas was her favorite. I'd been told that Dad was Grandfather's favorite, but Grandfather died fairly young, well before I was born.

The hardest part of summer was telling Grandmother and Uncle Thomas goodbye. They made the time Derrick and I spent at Dad's very special and memorable. When we returned home, I always looked forward to seeing them again.

Life with Mom was very different than life with Dad. Mom grew up the daughter of a Baptist minister, and I would see her read her Bible and talk to God, or pray, daily. She was such a great example for me.

After she left Dad, times were really difficult financially. Mom still had my older half-brother, Wayne, at home, as well as Derrick and me. Mom had nowhere else to go, so we moved in with her half-sister, Nancy, for a while. Aunt Nancy also had a strong faith in God, so Mom and Aunt Nancy would pray together for countless hours.

Mom said that God always provided because she asked for what she needed. When we had very little money and needed a car, Mom found one for $300. Then one day, Aunt Nancy put Mom in touch with a friend who had a trailer that was empty. This friend allowed us to live in the trailer rent-free. On another occasion, Mom ran out of laundry detergent and asked God to provide some so that she could wash clothes. Although she worked four jobs, she did not have the money to buy laundry detergent. We were amazed when, the next day, we found laundry detergent sitting on our doorstep. Mom smiled, firmly believing God would always provide for our needs.

After Mom and Dad divorced, Mom asked God to send the right man for her. After two failed marriages, Mom was tired of being with what she called "ungodly" men. "I prayed every night for nine months," she told me.

Mom reconnected with a friend she'd known since middle school. She and her friend Gary had even dated briefly in high school before going their own ways. Gary was divorced with two children of his own.

Mom and Gary were married shortly after they reconnected. Trying to balance five children was not easy, especially because Gary's children had hoped that he and their mom would reconcile. We had a lot of ups and downs in trying to blend into one family. We learned how to all tolerate one another, but it wasn't until we were all much older that we began to get along.

One day, Mom was sitting at the table, having just finished reading her Bible. She was preparing to eat, when she felt God telling her not to eat. For the next week, every time she started to eat anything, she said, she felt God telling her not to.

"God fulfills me," she said, and she was never hungry. She lived off of water and crackers that week.

One evening we all gathered on the narrow staircase for our family prayer time. In our tiny townhome in Austin, Texas, we sat listening to Mom talk to God. The room was dimly lit, but there was a window at the top of the stairs that allowed a minute amount of sunlight to stream through. As I sat listening to her talk and watched the light gather on the walls, I felt close to God. I had seen Mom spend time reading and praying to God. I knew the story of God's son, Jesus, coming to earth to die for the bad things I'd done. Suddenly it all made sense. I wanted to ask Jesus to be a part of my life.

I closed my eyes, and at 8 years old, I said, "Jesus, please come into my heart."

"I accepted Jesus as my Savior," I told Mom after I'd finished. She came to me, sat on the stairs beside me and wrapped her arms around me in a hug. Holding my hand, Mom and I prayed together, and I knew without a doubt Jesus was in my heart. I enjoyed the privacy we had on the staircase at that moment as I sat against the wall and we talked about God.

Mom had more to celebrate before the week was over. Derrick, Gary and Gary's son, Jack, all decided to ask Jesus to be part of their lives by the time Mom began to eat again.

By my freshman year of high school, I no longer wanted to go to Dad's. I would talk to him when he called, but that was our only communication. Though I didn't want to spend time with Dad, I regretted the time I missed with Grandmother.

Derrick visited Dad for another year, but he stopped going after they got into an argument that escalated to the point that Dad actually threatened to kill him. Whether it was an empty threat in the heat of the moment or not, that fight caused Derrick to cut ties with Dad permanently.

I met my lifelong best friend, Jenny, in athletics class when I was just 14. She invited me to her youth group where I became very involved. This was a time of significant spiritual growth for me and where our friendship blossomed into an unbreakable bond.

I strongly believed in saving sex for the sanctity of marriage. My beliefs were so strong that I even spoke to my youth group about the subject and practiced abstinence throughout high school. Cody, who was in the youth group, really appreciated my beliefs. We dated a year before he broke things off suddenly. I was devastated. I already felt distant from my dad, and breaking up with

Cody just emphasized the pain and my belief that I couldn't trust men. But I had no idea how much Dad would hurt everyone in the near future.

"I need to talk to you about something," Mom surprised me one January afternoon. She'd just returned from visiting her sister, Lisa. She had the strangest look on her face. There was a mixture of sadness and confusion in her eyes. All I knew was she didn't look like herself.

"What's wrong?" I asked. I was sitting in a chair at the end of the kitchen table, Mom standing in front of me, Gary and Derrick behind me.

"Your dad and Uncle Thomas got into an argument," Mom began. "Your dad pulled a gun out of his truck."

Dad always kept a gun in his truck for protection, I thought.

"He shot your uncle twice in the back," she said softly.

My heart stopped. I felt like I couldn't breathe. Her words seemed farther away, and I could barely focus.

"They were in the church parking lot, near Grandmother's house. Dad had pulled in to talk to the new minister, and Uncle Thomas pulled up to talk with him."

"Is Uncle Thomas okay?" I asked in shock and disbelief. Tears started running down my cheeks.

Mom shook her head. "He died on the way to the hospital."

I felt so many emotions at once. The sadness squeezed my heart tight. I sat at the table and cried with my family. *How am I even supposed to feel right now?*

I had so many questions that no one could answer. *What were they arguing about this time? What could Uncle Thomas possibly have said to make Dad so angry? Did he really think murder would solve his problems?*

We learned about the incident mostly through the media and the trial that followed. News reports stated Dad and Uncle Thomas were in an argument over a water bill. My uncle was not even armed. He was walking back to his truck when Dad shot him in the back. Dad drove back to his house and called the police on himself.

"He was threatening my life," Dad told the officers when they arrived.

We still don't know the whole story. All I know is that Dad left his family grief-stricken.

Three months later, Grandmother passed away. "She was heartbroken," one of my half-sisters on Dad's side told us. "She kept saying, 'I can't believe one son is dead and another is in prison.'"

I begged to go to Grandmother's funeral, but Mom felt it was unwise. Grandmother was very affectionate and had many friends who loved her. Her funeral was packed with people, and I was crushed that I couldn't go. I never got to say goodbye.

When the trial neared, Mom let us know that Derrick and I wouldn't be going. Mom, however, was subpoenaed to testify.

"They're giving her a really tough time," Gary said after her first day of testifying. "She's being attacked from both sides. The prosecution is using her to testify against him, and the defense is using her to testify for him, and it's tearing her apart."

"She'll lie and make me look bad," Dad told everyone and anyone who would listen.

The stress of the trial sent Mom into a time of bad depression.

Derrick and I didn't have to testify because we were minors, but my older half-sisters and half-brother were called to testify because they were adults. The strain on my family was intense.

Dad's trial ended, and he was sentenced to 32 years in prison. He was 59 years old when he was sentenced. I was sure he would never be released. Any hopes of a relationship with Dad were gone.

I grew very depressed after Dad shot Uncle Thomas. I felt very lonely and found myself willing to do anything to drive the loneliness away. I tried pot, but didn't like it very much, so I took up drinking. I liked the way drinking helped me avoid dealing with my feelings. I drank for a couple of years, but finally decided I did not like how sick I became and eventually gave it up.

I was 17 when my friend Jo invited me to her birthday party and introduced me to her school friend Anthony. I could finally see a bright spot in the darkness I was going through. There was just something about him. We instantly clicked. He loved to be silly and made me laugh. I had a great time with him, and he made me forget all the pain I was going through.

"I wish Dad were here," I told Mom when I graduated high school. "He always encouraged me to do well in school."

I looked up at the board with all the graduates' names. I looked at my last name and thought about Dad. I was so sad that he was not there for my big day.

My loneliness only increased after I graduated high school. I decided sex was no longer worth the wait. I had a friend Brett, and we decided to just "get it over with."

Cody, then in college, called me when he learned about Brett and me. Cody was terribly disappointed that I had not waited until I was married, the way I had vowed. He had decided he wanted to marry me, but I turned him down. He had hurt me badly, and I wasn't willing to give him another chance.

I was looking for someone and something to fill a growing void inside of me. I convinced myself that I could fill this vacancy with men and the physical act of love.

I had two consecutive relationships with men I met at work. Daniel and Steven were both mysterious, and that was attractive to me. I lived with each for about a year before breaking up.

I thought that love would solve my problems, but it

didn't. I did not really attend church or spend time with God the way I should. Steven constantly argued with me that there was no God. I tried to defend my faith, but wasn't completely sure how to go about expressing my beliefs.

Mom would ask me questions to make me think about my relationships. "I just didn't feel he was right for you," Mom honestly told me after each guy.

"Why?"

"Did he have a relationship with God?"

"No."

"Did sex before marriage help the relationship?"

"No." I hated to admit it. I wanted Mom's approval. This was a common conversation Mom and I had about all of my boyfriends. Mom only wanted the best for me.

"I want you to value yourself the way God does, and save yourself for marriage," Mom reminded me.

Anthony, the friend I'd made at Jo's party, was there for me after every breakup. He knew I was heartbroken. I grew deeply depressed — even to the point of avoiding food. My doctor eventually put me on medicine to deal with my depression.

Anthony continued to be my friend through all of the ups and downs of my relationships. I was working hard and going to college, and I felt so alone. "What am I going to do?" I would cry on his shoulder while he listened to me intently.

"You're the strongest person I know," he'd tell me, wrapping me into his arms for a hug.

"Go to church with me," I begged Anthony one day. We began attending church together and grew closer. In many ways, we grew up — out of being teenagers and into adulthood — with one another.

"I really care for you," Anthony surprised me by saying one day. "I don't want to scare you. I just need you to know that I really value our relationship and can't imagine life without you."

"Uhhh … yeah …" I was left speechless. I stared into his hazel eyes and saw the sincerity in them. I didn't know what to say. "I just want to be friends," I admitted. I didn't want to ruin how well our relationship worked by taking it to the next level. I was scared to admit — even to myself — that he might be the one.

Five years after Dad was sentenced, Mom surprised me with more news. "Your dad has been granted a new trial."

I stared at her in disbelief. "Why would they want a new trial?"

"Something about the entire police tapes were not played in the first one," she said. "I'm not entirely sure."

"Are you afraid?" I asked her. After his first trial, she had been terrified of him. She knew how angry he must be, and she was afraid of what he might do to her for testifying against him.

"I was, but I've prayed and prayed about it for years.

I'm not afraid of him any longer," she admitted. "God took away my fear."

I thought back to when he was first incarcerated. He had been filled with hate and anger and vowed to seek revenge on everyone who testified against him.

When he first went to prison, I wanted to correspond with him. I wanted to get to know Dad as a person.

"If you could go anywhere in the world, where would you go?" I asked when I wrote him. I wanted to learn who he was and what he enjoyed.

"I need you to send me money. I need shoes and some shirts. I don't want people to think I'm poor while I'm in here," was the typical response I received to all questions. After a few tries, I stopped writing him.

Now he'd been moved back to the county jail for his new trial. "While he's near here waiting for his retrial, I think I'm going to see Dad. Maybe I can get some answers to my questions," I told Derrick and Mom. Dad had to provide a list of people who could come see him or you weren't allowed into the jail.

Entering the jail was intimidating. There were no doors except the entry and exit. The building was old and smelled moldy and stuffy. I felt sick and sad that this was where Dad had ended up.

I walked down the long hallway to the visitors' area and saw Dad sitting behind a pane of glass in his prison suit. He looked like a stranger. His hair had turned white, his body had thinned and he had aged a lot.

I wanted to hug him immediately through the glass. I

pulled up my seat and lifted the phone from the hook in order to talk with Dad as tears rolled down my face. He was shorter than me now, as it had been nine years since I had seen him.

"Are you sorry for what you did?" I asked.

"I was scared for my life."

"Are you sad Uncle Thomas died?"

"He's the one who kept threatening me."

"He wasn't even armed."

"How do I know he wouldn't have been when he reached his car?"

"Aren't you sad you didn't get to go to your mother's funeral?"

He just stared back at me. I was saddened he didn't even care.

"Are you sad you missed watching your children and grandchildren grow up?" I couldn't help but sob with the sorrow I felt.

"Yes, but what I did was right," he said flatly. "How is school?"

Dad loved to change the subject. I wanted to scream, "Why can't you just own up to what you did?!" But I didn't.

"Fine." I sighed in frustration.

"I want you to make sure you get good grades."

"I will. I want you to know I love you, Dad."

"I love you, too, Emma."

"I forgive you for what you did."

"I didn't do anything wrong," he said.

My heart was overflowing with sadness. Our 30-minute visit was up, and I had so many more questions. Tears fell down our cheeks as we put our palms to the glass to say goodbye. As soon as I reached the other side of the doors, I allowed the sobs to rack my body for Dad and the man he'd become.

His sentence was reduced to 12.5 years at the end of the second trial. I realized I was going to have to decide if I wanted a relationship with Dad when he was released. In the meantime, I didn't want to think about it. I just wanted to enjoy life and find love.

I thought I'd found the solution to my loneliness and quest for love when Jo introduced me to James later that year. When we first met, I wasn't interested, but James persisted until I caved.

Our first date was a birthday dinner for a friend of his from work. After we finished eating, James took me back to his house and gave me the grand tour.

"This is really nice," I told him. He had been building the one-story brick house, and it was almost finished. I loved the little front porch, the big tree in the front yard and the quiet location. It wasn't long before I moved in with him.

A month after we started dating, I discovered he'd given me an incurable STD. I was angry at James for not telling me. *If our relationship is going to continue,* I thought, *we have some serious trust issues to work through.*

I had a close friend, Kate, who had also gone through a similar experience and was a lifeline for me. It was nice to talk with someone who really understood.

James and I had a lot to work through, but we decided to work at it together. We had a lot of good times spent with friends on Lake Travis where James taught me to drive his boat and eat crawfish. I really appreciated his support and encouragement to go to college and pursue an education.

On the Fourth of July, James took me to a place with a view over Lake Travis.

"We have been a rock for each other through everything," James startled me by saying right before the fireworks were expected to begin. I was surprised when he bent down on his knee.

"Will you marry me?" he asked, holding up an engagement ring.

"Yes!" I exclaimed with rolling tears.

"Things will only get better from here on out," he promised, pulling me into his arms. I inhaled the smell of the clean soap he wore. I held onto this promise when things were bad between us. I had no idea how difficult they were about to become.

The next month, I was cooking dinner while I waited for James to come home from work.

I put the pan on the stove and turned the grease on low. While the grease heated, I ran into the bathroom and turned the water on. I wanted it to run over the paint roller I'd been using that day before the paint dried. I was gone less than a minute, but when I walked back into the kitchen, I froze in horror. The cabinets were on fire, and smoke filled the room. I knelt on my hands and knees and began to crawl toward the door, while looking for the dog. I had to make sure I got the dog out.

Then I ran back to the stove and grabbed the pan, throwing it into the sink to stop the fire. When I threw the pan, grease splattered down my body, burning my clothes and skin.

Somehow I made it outside and called 911. I tried to call James but couldn't reach him.

"What are you doing out here?" James called out to me when he pulled up the driveway moments later and saw me standing in the street on the phone. I pointed to the house. I couldn't even find the words to speak. The cabinets were still on fire, and smoked billowed out from the windows. James jumped out of his truck. He grabbed a bucket and filled it with water, rushed into the kitchen and put the fire out. The fire trucks pulled up as he put the last of the fire out.

I had suffered second-degree burns down my right leg, foot and left arm. My foot swelled, which made it difficult to walk. James helped me to keep my foot propped up and to hop around on crutches while it healed. We faced some difficult months of recovery, both for my burns and the house. We were thrilled months later when I had recovered and we had finished restoring the kitchen. I continued to hold onto that promise that life would get better.

But by our wedding date that summer, James was frustrated and wasn't even sure if he wanted to be married. While I wore an amazing ivory lace wedding dress with a V-neck front and back, in a fitted trump style that flowed behind me, James wore shorts and flip-flops. We were married at the lake near where we lived.

After the wedding, neither one of us was happy. I did everything to try to please James. I jumped to fulfill his every need, even if it was just to fill up his drink in the evening. I grew frustrated when he would not talk to me or share his day with me. Before long, we were hardly speaking to each other.

I felt I had nowhere to turn. "Will it always be like this?" I asked God. "What am I supposed to do? I don't know how much more I can take!" I cried out.

One day, my Bible fell open to Proverbs 3, and I began to read: "Trust in the Lord with all your heart and lean not on your own understanding. In all your ways submit to him, and he will make your paths straight."

"I have to focus on God and not try to figure things out," I constantly reminded myself.

I talked to God. I would tell him how lonely I was while I cleaned. I spent a lot of time cleaning to deal with my pain. None of my friends or family could understand why James would not talk with me and comforted me by explaining that my marriage could be saved if we would work on it.

Mom began to pray during this time for her children to have spouses who loved God and spent time reading the Bible.

One night James was sitting at the table, and I sat down across from him. "I've been working on me. I may need counseling with issues I've had with Dad. You've been distant and quiet lately. What's going on?"

We sat in silence for a while before James answered. "I think we're over. I want a divorce."

"What? Why?" I sobbed. "Are you that miserable?" He didn't offer an explanation.

I returned to my mom's house that night. I was heartbroken. I'd thought James was different than the other men I'd been with.

A few weeks later, I returned to the house and discovered that Tracy, James' ex-fiancé, had moved her belongings in immediately after I moved out. This devastated me, and I screamed at James.

"How could you?" I kept screaming at him. "What changed after we married?" I asked, but James never gave me an answer.

We were divorced after seven months of marriage, and James and Tracy married before the end of the year.

"I'm so angry!" I sat on my bed and cried out to God. "Why did you let this happen to me?" Confused and hurt after my divorce, I struggled to find answers.

I opened my Bible and read Jeremiah 29:11. "'For I know the plans I have for you,' declares the Lord, 'plans to prosper you and not to harm you, plans to give you hope and a future.'"

I was very depressed and spent most of my time alone, but I found myself clinging to this promise from God I found in Jeremiah. I spent a lot of time in prayer and studying the Bible.

One night, while staring out the big window of my apartment, I decided to pull out a sheet of paper. I began to write. I wrote the name of every man I'd ever had a sexual relationship with.

"I'm giving this to you, Lord." I raised the sheet up in the air. "I tried to do these things for me. I thought they would help. They did nothing for me. I'm asking for your forgiveness. I want to start over," I said. "I don't know what the future holds. I'm scared and alone. I want to be married. I don't want this pain any longer. Please send me a godly husband."

I began to really focus on and renew my relationship with God. I read my Bible, prayed and went to church. Slowly, I began to heal.

"Would you like to go on a women's retreat?" Kate asked me, not long after my divorce. "This is a once-in-a-lifetime opportunity," she said, smiling. "You can only go on this particular retreat once in your life."

I was lavished with love for the three days we were there. I stepped out of my comfort zone to share my life story with the other women.

I couldn't believe how open and transparent we all were with one another.

The next evening we were listening to an audio speech. I had my head bowed on the table, resting, when I heard a voice call, *Emma ... Emma!* I looked up, but all of the other women were also resting. No one was looking at me.

I felt like God was speaking to me!

"God, thank you for showing me you are real and have not left me all alone," I prayed.

Before the retreat was over, we returned to our rooms to find a bag left on our bunk beds. I opened my bag to discover more than 60 cards and letters from family and friends. They had all kept this beautiful surprise from me for the previous few months, as they wrote and submitted these written reminders of why they loved me and how much I meant to them.

I couldn't stop crying as I read the cards. I was overwhelmed with the love and support I felt from everyone I knew.

A year and a half after my divorce, Anthony's long-term relationship ended.

"Should we cross the friendship line?" we asked one another and ourselves. We decided to take the leap toward romance and began dating.

Anthony was and is so different from any man I've dated and from my dad. We go to church together, study the Bible together and pray together. We've agreed to save sex for marriage. I know that God has given me Anthony to spend the rest of my life with.

Not long ago, Anthony and I began to pray about a church to attend. When our friend Sydney invited us to visit Believers Church, we agreed. From the moment we walked in the front doors, everyone was so loving and welcoming to us. We felt like we were home.

Pastor RJ is straightforward and exudes the love of God. You can feel the love he has for his church family. He isn't there to put on a show. He's there to love people and share his love for God with others.

At Believers Church, we feel wanted, welcomed and loved.

"I'm keeping tabs on what is going on in the area," Dad wrote to me a few months ago. "I've forgiven those who testified against me. When I get out, maybe I'll travel to the Philippines and Mexico and around the world. After all, I'm going to sue the government and win restitution for the time I was in prison. I should win a couple of billion dollars in my suit. Then I can go to the Philippines and Mexico and start my own business."

Dad has grand dreams about life after his release. He teaches classes in prison and says he is doing well. I worry that he's still very angry and that he'll have a tough time when he gets out.

I find myself praying about what God would have me do about having a relationship with him after his release. I'm sure that God has used my journey to set me on the course he has planned for my life. He's sent me people like Mom, Jenny, Kate and Anthony to help me through the rough times. I'm so thankful for Anthony, and most importantly, I'm thankful for the relationship he has with God. Because of not wanting to repeat my pattern of tumultuous relationships, I've learned to seek God in everything I do.

I found out that the only thing that could fill the void Dad and other men left in my life was God. I know now that God loves me unconditionally, and I can live with the confidence that he has a plan for me. With God's help, I was even able to come off all of my depression medication.

Because of Jesus, I am whole, healthy and loved. Because of the assurance I have that God loves *me*, I'm learning day by day to forgive and love my dad.

Isle of Hope

The Story of Annie

Written by Arlene Showalter

"Chase!" I strode toward our best friend's SUV. Maybe he could tell me where to find my son, Levi. I rushed around to the driver's side. No Chase. *Why'd he leave his engine running?* I wondered, as I peered through the darkly tinted windows. My heart pounded as I tapped on the window.

The car moved around like a bear was trapped inside. One blackened window cracked open.

"Hi, Chase." I felt a surge of relief. "I'm looking for Levi. Have you seen him?"

"Just a minute." The window shut, and the car rocked some more.

Finally, my pre-teen son emerged from the backseat, tucking his shirttail in his jeans. I started to get a bad feeling. He hunched his shoulders and stared at his sneakers.

"Hi, Mom."

"Hey, whatcha doing for the next 50 years?" The cute maintenance man in coveralls flashed a brilliant smile.

I fumbled with my timecard, ready to punch out from working as a ward clerk in the local hospital, while my mind whirled, not knowing how to respond to such a question from a complete stranger.

"Name's Allen." He stuck out a hand.

"Annie."

"You going to college around here? What year?"

I giggled. "I just graduated from high school back in Colorado. My sister lives here."

"Then you are in need of some good Texas friends!" he said, grinning.

A few months later, he asked me out. I agreed and soon learned Allen was studying for a degree in industrial technology when he wasn't mopping highly polished floors. Over the next few weeks, he made a point to stop by and see me. He proved as steady and precise as his field when we married two years later.

"My boss has offered me a new job," Allen announced a year after his graduation.

"Wonderful!"

"Well, wonderful depends on whether you mind moving to Atlanta," he said.

"Wherever you go, I go." I smiled. "Just like Ruth and Naomi in the Bible."

"I'll take you up on that." Allen grinned. "A new adventure for our new lives together."

"We should find a church to call home," I suggested soon after our move. We had gone to several, but couldn't find one that seemed like a good fit.

"How about that one?" Allen said. A sign pointed to a church that met inside a small shopping strip just a short drive from our house.

"Couldn't hurt. Let's go."

"Good morning." The pastor of the storefront congregation approached. "I'm Edwin, and this is my wife, Ruth."

"Good morning."

"You folks from around here?"

"No, we just moved from Texas. Allen got a job here in Atlanta."

"No kidding. We're from Texas, too." Ed grinned. "How about coming home for lunch after the service?"

"Have you hiked in the mountains yet?" Ed asked.

"No."

"You haven't lived until you've experienced North Georgia waterfalls."

"Far from here?" I asked.

"Not at all. Amicalola Falls is about 90 minutes northwest, and Anna Ruby Falls about 90 minutes northeast. We love going to them both. The hike in is short but beautiful, and both falls are spectacular. Ruth and I get up there as often as we can."

"The beauty of creation puts all of life back into perspective," Ruth added. "We always come back refreshed and reminded that God is in control."

"Edwin and Ruth are so real," I said to Allen after another weekend jaunt to Anna Ruby Falls. He sat on the bed and unlaced his boots.

"How so?"

"Don't you think it's amazing how they talk about God like he's their best friend? I've been a Christian for years, but I've never experienced God as they do."

"I agree. When we sit, talking, at their dinner table, I sometimes look around to see if Jesus is sitting there, too."

"I want to know Jesus at that level," I said.

"For sure," Allen echoed.

"I have some women coming over for a Bible study," Ruth told me. "Would you like to join us?"

"Yes, I'd love to."

We studied the book of Revelation, and I had a revelation of my own. Bible prophecy was fascinating to me, especially what the ancients wrote about the end times — the natural calamities and chaos and wars that will come before the end of the world.

I realized what the goal of my faith was all about — being able to be with Jesus face to face and to spend eternity with him.

Somehow God used that study to change my whole perspective on life. I believed the return of Jesus could be any time. I wanted to be ready, and I wanted to share that hope with everyone I knew.

God put me on this earth to really know him and to make him known to others, I realized. *He has a specific plan and purpose for my life, and I want to fulfill that purpose.*

Deep thoughts ran through my mind as I drove home from another study. "God," I prayed. "It seems I've known *about* you for years, but not really *known* you like Ed and Ruth do. I accept that Jesus died for me on the cross, and he's my Savior, but now I realize there's more to it than that. You are seeking disciples, not converts. I want to know you more. I want to walk closely with you every day. Right here, right now, I choose to submit my life to you and will seek to follow you all of my life."

"My cousin Luke has offered me a partnership in his business," Allen told me, three years after our move to Atlanta. "But we'd have to move back to Texas."

"That sounds like an offer too good to pass up," I told him.

"It'll take us back to family, too."

"And since Ed and Ruth already moved back to Texas, we would be a little closer to them," I added. "I think we should do it."

We moved to Austin so Allen could start up a branch office to his cousin's in Corpus Christi. He also returned to school to earn the engineering degree he'd need when Luke made him full partner. I helped with the office work, while Allen built up the business. However, that promised partnership proved more elusive than spilled mercury.

"He'll come through," Allen promised, many times. "He says there are complications right now. He's my cousin. Luke wouldn't lie to me."

"Let's drive down this road," I suggested as we returned home one day after a birthday party, with our kids in tow.

"Okay." Allen turned down the back road.

"Look at that cute house!" I pointed at the small white clapboard house with a screened-in front porch.

"Has a For Sale sign."

"Looks like a good piece of land comes with it, too. Let's check it out."

Allen pulled into the driveway. "Looks abandoned."

We all piled out of the car and began strolling through the waist-high grass.

"Look, honeysuckle is growing everywhere!"

"Wow, I think this is a peach tree!"

"And here's a plum tree."

"Come down here!" our son shouted. "A rock wall — and water!"

We all raced to the stream and listened to the water burbling over boulders snuggled in the creek bed. As one, we all tossed shoes and socks aside and dug our toes into the sandy bottom.

"This place is fantastic," I said. "Let's call on it." We figured it would be way over our budget. Even though it was rundown, it was a beautiful setting.

The real estate agent informed us that more than 30 people had tried to buy the house, and every sale had fallen through. "The owner is very motivated to sell," he told Allen. "As a matter of fact, he just lowered the price today!"

We put our house on the market as soon as we got home and amazingly had two offers within the first week. The seller allowed us to rent the country house until ours closed.

"Talk about God's goodness. I think he saved this place just for us."

We all moved into the two-bedroom trailer situated on the back portion of the property and spent the next three and a half years remodeling and adding onto the 50-year-old farmhouse. Allen did all the work himself while still juggling work and school.

We laid a new foundation, added rooms, moved walls, updated the electrical and plumbing and installed a new roof.

The older kids chased each other on rollerblades, while our newborn daughter swung on the front porch in her little swing. The 15 acres offered lots of exploration for the kids as well, while Allen and I hammered away.

"We're big on people gathering in small groups," the pastor of our church in Texas told us. "I would like you to join Chase and Carol Brown's group. Chase is a strong Christian leader, and you can learn a lot from his example."

We met the Browns and were delighted to learn they had two boys the same ages as our own, 7 and 4, whom they homeschooled.

"You should try homeschooling," Carol said. "You'd love it. You have so much more freedom with scheduling and courses."

"And you can make sure your children grow up with solid Christian principles," Chase added.

"It's certainly worth a try, if you're up to it," Allen said, when we discussed it later.

We settled into the perfect American dream life. We tripled the size of our house while acquiring many farm animals: horses, chickens, goats, cows, pigs, rabbits, birds, dogs and cats. I homeschooled the children, while Allen worked and remodeled the house on the weekends. Our lives were full and happy.

"God is so good," I exclaimed when we left the Browns' home after another group gathering. "I've missed Ed and Ruth so much since we came back to Texas, and now he's given us Chase and Carol. Our boys are the same age, and it's so wonderful how Chase takes the time to take the four boys mountain biking so often. And we have this wonderful home, too."

"Yes, God certainly provides," Allen agreed.

The group grew to about 20 people, and we became very close. We accepted Chase's capable leadership and adored his wife. She and I became best friends, discussing God, church, children and life.

"I think our group should start meeting on Sundays, too," Chase said, looking around at his devoted flock. "We don't need to go to a big church where it's so impersonal. Let's just have church in one another's homes."

"Sounds great," several agreed.

We grew even closer under Chase's guidance. We mountain biked along the trails and back roads of our region, prayed together, camped, worshipped, studied, vacationed together and grew ever tighter.

Chase's sons and our sons became like brothers, staying at one another's homes on weekends.

I stood on my porch and watched the guys take off for another biking jaunt, kicking up dust under their tires. *God, thank you so much for this wonderful land, the creek, the animals and our wonderful friends.*

Some contented years passed. Because of Allen's heavy schedule, we dropped out of the home group, but we kept in close contact with Chase and Carol through homeschooling activities. Later, we found a church closer to home and attended occasionally. The pastor, Mr. Bentley, treated us with complete loving acceptance and never judged us for our long absences from church.

"Can you drive me to the doctor's office?" Mom asked me around Christmas of 2002.

Dad had taken her to the emergency room because of abnormal bleeding, and they immediately scheduled a hysterectomy. The procedure revealed that Mom had stage 4 cancer which had already spread to her stomach and bladder.

"Do you want to go through chemotherapy treatment?" the doctor asked.

Mom shook her head. "No. I lost a son to cancer. I saw what chemo did to him."

"Are you sure, Mom?" I asked.

"I'm ready to go," she said. "Don't worry. I'll be with Jesus. What could be better than that?"

Mom eventually went through a series of chemo treatments, but it became apparent it wasn't helping, and she had to stop.

I shared her health issues with my pastor and his wife.

"God won't heal her if she doesn't have faith," Pastor Mitch said. He'd replaced our older, beloved Pastor Bentley a short time before.

"I have the faith *for* her," I said. "I'll believe God's promises for healing, even if she can't or doesn't."

Mom continued creeping toward her rendezvous with God.

"Listen to me," she said. "I appreciate your fasting and praying for my healing, but if it doesn't happen, don't you ever let anyone tell you that you didn't have enough faith."

"But, Mom, God has promised healing. Look at Psalm

118:17. 'I will not die but live, and will proclaim what the Lord has done.'"

"If I go, then it's my time to go. Never forget that."

"But 1 Peter promises that 'by his wounds you are healed.'"

"I'll be fine, dear. Truly, I will."

Mom's rapid decline lay heavy on my heart. One day, our ladies prayer meeting had canceled, so rather than go straight home, I decided to pop in on my kids to see how they were doing. The homeschool group gathered twice a week in a local church so the kids could attend various classes. Parents were always welcome to come and sit in. I walked to Levi's class and slipped in. No Levi.

That's strange. Where in the world is he?

I went back outside and started walking through the parking lot and along some of the trails where the kids liked to walk during their lunch break. No Levi.

I continued to the rear of the parking lot.

There's Chase's SUV. What's he doing here? Maybe he knows where Levi is.

I approached the car and heard the motor running. I peered through the front windshield. No Chase. *This is really weird.*

I peered through the side windows, but couldn't see anything through the heavy tint, so I began tapping on the glass. I heard scrambling, and finally Chase's eyes appeared through the window he'd cracked open.

"What is going on?" I asked. "I'm looking for Levi." I

heard more commotion from the rear of the SUV. "Do you know where he is?"

Another thump from the vehicle.

"Is Levi in there with you?"

"Uh, yeah. We, um, we're going mountain biking," Chase stuttered.

"During class time? Where are the bikes? Why's he in the car with you?"

"Well, we, um, we had to change clothes for biking."

I stood and waited. Finally, Levi emerged from the backseat, tucking his shirt into his pants.

"Come with me," I said, taking my 12-year-old son by the hand. "We're going back to class."

Once inside, I turned and led Levi into the darkened auditorium.

"Levi, what is going on?" I asked, while fear gnawed at my stomach. I watched terror fill his eyes and sweat form on his brow.

"You need to tell me."

Silence.

"Are you okay?"

More silence. I inhaled, deep and slow. "I'm going to take you back to class now."

After I left him in class, I turned and walked toward the front doors. Chase passed me in the hallway.

"Is everything okay?" he asked.

"Yes."

"Is Levi in class?"

"Yes." That was the last time I ever saw Chase.

My stomach roiled, but I maintained my gait toward the exit and the fresh air it promised. I reached the private haven of my car, got in and locked the doors. Sobs heaved and rolled on this sea of unexplained, unknown terror. I willed my fingers still as I called Allen.

"I don't know what's going on," I sobbed, "but something horrible just happened."

"What?"

"I'm not sure, but I think Levi and Chase were naked in Chase's car."

"Bring the kids home now," Allen said. "I'll meet you there."

"I have to talk to you." I had called Carol. "Meet me at the coffee house."

After she arrived, I nervously fiddled with my cup. *How do I tell my best friend that I think her husband has been molesting our son?* I swallowed hard and presented my suspicions.

"If he *did*, I'll have to press charges," I said. "I'm so sorry."

Carol remained silent. Her face registered no shock. Or surprise. Or anger.

I returned home more confused than ever.

After the other children had gone to bed, Allen and I went into Levi's bedroom. Allen put his arm around his son and pulled him close. "We have to know what's been going on."

Levi's body stiffened, and he stared at the floor.

"Whatever's happened, it's not your fault. You are not in trouble."

Silence.

"Were you naked in Chase's car today?"

A slight nod.

"Did — did Chase touch you?"

Another nod.

"Was this the first time?"

A slight shake.

We called the police to press charges. My mind scrambled like Texas tumbleweed as Allen let the officers in the front door. *Our best friend! A leader in the church! How is it possible?*

Carol called me the next day. "Chase has disappeared." She paused. "And there's a piece to this puzzle that you don't know about. Years ago he spent time in jail for sexual molestation of a child."

"*What?* Are you kidding me?" I blurted. "You knew his history and made no effort to protect my son from him? How could you?"

My world spun out of control. We learned that many people knew of Chase's secret, and nobody, *nobody*, made a move to protect our son from his prowling ways.

Three days after I discovered Levi's secret, the police found Chase's body. He'd ended his nightmare with a bullet — while ours was just beginning.

Mom's condition worsened. I tried to get her to understand and embrace God's promises of healing. Finally, after she entered hospice care, I accepted what she'd tried to get me to understand.

"It's okay to go be with Jesus, Mom," I said, bending low over her. "I love you." Dad, my sister and I all softly sang "Amazing Grace," while Mom slipped into eternity.

"If you had the faith of a mustard seed," Mitch intoned, "you could move this mountain."

He's blaming us for Mom's death. Her words came back, *"Don't let anyone tell you I died for lack of faith. If it's my time, it's my time."*

"Ask whatever you will, and I will grant it," Mitch quoted. His eyes seemed to pierce through me and pin me to the back wall.

God, we need your help. Our closest and dearest friends deceived and betrayed us. Levi lost his buddies and his innocence. Mom died even though I prayed for healing, and now I feel the pastor is blaming us. I can't take it.

"We need counseling," I told Allen soon after Mom's death. "We've lost our best friends. Levi lost his best friends. His trust has been violated. Mine is shattered. I don't think I can survive this without outside help."

"I agree."

We found a wonderful counselor, David, and went for private and family sessions.

"The first thing you need to do is quit homeschooling," David advised.

"Why? Our children love it."

"Because you need to get Levi into a whole new environment. Think about it. Everywhere he goes, he sees and remembers the events Chase forced upon him. He needs a fresh start."

We found a small private school that readily received our broken family with open arms.

"I'm fine," Levi insisted as I drove him to another session with David. "I don't need to keep talking about this."

"David says you are making progress, but you're not quite ready to stop yet."

Levi folded his arms across his chest and stuck his chin out. But he went. And we learned more of the extent of the abuse. More than we wanted to believe.

"It's worse than we thought," Allen told me after a private session with David.

"How much worse?" Allen's silence said it all. The abuse had been going on for three years of his young life.

"No, God, no!" I screamed. I fled outside, trying to outrun the truth, and dropped to my knees, screaming and screaming.

Allen followed me and bent over my prostrate body. "Please," he begged. "The kids will hear you."

I didn't care about Allen. Or the kids. Or God. I only cared that my son had been violated and betrayed. "How, how?" I wailed. "My son. My son. No. No. No."

"Luke's never going to make me partner in his business," Allen told me two years later. Allen had worked hard to build up a very successful business and had faithfully given 15 years of his life to the company. "Luke finally came clean and admitted it. He tried to toss me some bonuses like a bone, but I told him I'm done."

"What will we do?"

"I've been looking around. Found a great opportunity in El Paso."

"That's 600 miles from here," I gasped. "We'll have to give up the farm."

"I'm sorry, honey, but I don't see any other way. Maybe new surroundings will help us all."

"I'll never move!" I was determined.

Allen flew west to interview and landed the job. I wandered over the property we'd loved and nurtured for 10 years.

"Who but us would ever appreciate the blood, sweat and tears we poured into that house?" Our children grew up there, and my mom was buried in the small cemetery next to our property. I sobbed, gazing at it through fresh tears.

"God, why, why would you make us leave this place

that you gave us? And why now, when we're still trying to rebuild our lives?"

We put the farm on the market and found an immediate buyer.

I guess this is what God wants. I tried to feel thankful, but failed.

Everything drastically changed about our lives. We moved from country to city, small church to huge church, private school to public school and were surrounded by a large Hispanic community. None of us spoke Spanish.

Isolation wrapped its icy fingers around my mind and heart — and squeezed. Allen, the children and I struggled to adapt.

I clung to God even more in those years that felt like exile.

"What will happen to Levi?" I cried out to God in the solitude of our home.

Annie, I will provide for you. You grieve now, but I will give Levi a crown of beauty instead of ashes. I will give you and Allen and Levi the oil of gladness instead of mourning, and a garment of praise instead of a spirit of despair. God personalized Isaiah 61:3 for me. *Trust me, Annie, Levi will be called an oak of righteousness. He is a planting of the Lord for the display of my splendor.*

"But, God, how will he ever recover? How can he ever forget?"

I will teach him who he is in me, God answered, *and his peace will be great* (Isaiah 54:13).

I searched the Bible for every verse that would bring

healing to my son and prayed each promise over and over again. My heart began the ongoing healing process, along with Levi's.

"The schools and the culture here are having too big of an impact on our kids," Allen said to me one night, five years after our move. "We need to do something. I want you and the kids to move back to our old farm. The kids can go back to the friends they know, and you will be in a much better environment. I have to stay here and work and will fly back as often as I can."

Our first buyer had backed out three days before closing, and we'd had a renter ever since.

Tears streamed down my face. "Not without you! It will be too hard to live apart. And the commute will be hard for you."

"I know, but we have to do what's best for our kids." I knew it was the right thing to do, but it took all I had to shake my head in agreement.

Although delighted to be back on our beloved farm, I missed Allen's presence. He came home every other weekend, but we'd never been apart so long before. The transition coming home was even harder than leaving it years before.

I feel like a single parent. I kicked at some stones in our yard. *I'm the only one here to help the kids with their schoolwork and take them to all their events.*

I'd returned to Mitch's church for reasons unknown to me and baffling to Allen.

"Why would you want to go back?" he'd asked.

"I don't know," I said, shrugging. "I guess I don't want to find another church without you, and besides, David told us its best not to tell too many people about Levi's trauma, until he is old enough to process it. Mitch already knows."

Allen had shrugged, too. "I'll support you, but it certainly wouldn't be my first choice."

I wandered down to our beloved stream and listened to the water's perpetual prattle against the rocks. I broke a twig in several pieces and dropped them into the water. They gyrated in tight swirls before the current dragged them toward their final destiny.

I miss Allen. I'm tired of sleeping alone at night and making so many decisions on my own. My thoughts spun like the broken twig. *I miss friends I can trust and a pastor who listens to my heart without judging me.*

Three years passed with Allen coming home every other weekend. "I can't take this!" I cried. "I feel so alone. So abandoned."

"But what can we do? Should I quit this job?"

"No, you can't do that."

"How about this." He took me in his arms and rested his chin on the top of my head. "I'll fly home every weekend. Will that help?"

"Yes." I squeezed him with all my strength. "Yes, yes, yes."

We had returned to the same church, even though Mitch continued his controlling ways. We remained faithful, but unfulfilled and unfed.

One day, I decided to take piano lessons, and someone recommended Donna. We hit it off immediately, and our student/teacher relationship quickly blossomed into a deep friendship. She helped me process my struggles and disappointments and would always bring me hope and encouragement.

Edwin and Ruth came to visit from North Carolina, where they were then living, and attended church with us. After the service, Ruth and I stood in the ladies room, talking. "You need to leave this church." Her adamant tone surprised me. "They are stifling you and hindering you from growing in real relationship with Jesus."

"I know, but we've invested years into this place. How can we just leave?" We helped with nearly every aspect of the church.

"Investment or no," she said, "where will you be in another 10 years? Look at you. You are so on edge, always trying to please this man. He's bullying you through manipulation and control."

"I'll think about it, I promise."

That night I sat my whole family down at the dining room table. "What would you say if I told you I think we need to leave this church?"

"Yes, yes!" I stared at my kids in amazement.

"I never understood why you stuck it out so long," Allen added.

"We have to find a new church," I told Donna during my next lesson.

"Why not come to mine?" she asked. I knew she led the worship team at Believers Church, and I longed for true worship. "No pressure. No strings."

"Okay."

"Next Sunday?"

"Next Sunday."

"You'll love the church." Donna grinned. "Especially the worship leader."

I laughed.

Although excited about my first visit to Believers Church, my heart argued its concerns. *God, I need discernment,* I prayed within myself. *I've been so deceived in other churches. I thought Chase was a man to respect, and look what he did to our family. And I'm so tired of Mitch's attitude and accusations. I really, really need to know that this is the church for us because I don't trust my own judgment.*

We walked in as the band warmed up.

"Welcome, I'm RJ." The smiling man greeted us with a warm handshake.

"Thank you. We're happy to be here," I said. "Donna invited us."

"This is my wife, Jody." He put his arm around a lady with large, serene eyes.

"So nice to meet you." Jody held out her hand. "Donna tells us you play the piano."

"A little. Not as well as Donna!"

It wasn't long before they invited me to worship practice. I was perplexed.

Say what? You hardly know me, and you're already offering to let me be a part of the team? For years, I was under such tight scrutiny that I was unable to really use the gifts that God had given me.

"God has given you these gifts and talents," RJ said. "Don't be afraid to use them."

RJ approached me some months later. "How would you like to help in our women's ministry?"

"I'd be honored, but are you sure?"

"Of course, why wouldn't I be?" Surprise flitted across his face.

"It's been a long time since anyone trusted me enough to use the gifts that God has given me."

"As I told you before," he said, smiling broadly, "this is God's house. You are free to be yourself, to learn with all of us about what it means to fall in love with Jesus and to teach others to do the same."

Two years have passed. Every time I gather with the worship team to begin another service, a genuine sense of acceptance rolls over me, like a tsunami of love — deep and enveloping. My heart begins to beat in cadence with our drummer.

Free at last. Free at last. Thank God Almighty, I'm free at last.

A New Song in My Heart

The Story of Denise

Written by Karen Koczwara

Nooo!

I stared at the ultrasound screen, a dark, black hole glaring back at me.

There is no baby.

Tears filled my eyes, blurring the devastating image on the screen. Time froze for a moment, my heart thudding in my chest as I lay on the cold little bed.

You were supposed to be my miracle baby, bringing my husband and me closer after all we've been through. Now, you are gone, taken from our lives before you gasped your first breath.

It just isn't fair!

My broken heart has just begun to mend, and now it's splitting in two once again. How much more can I take?

I was born in Holland in March 1980. When I turned 2, we moved to London, where my father continued work in the oil business. My younger brother was born later that year, and when I turned 4, we relocated halfway around the world to California.

My early years held all the promise of an idyllic life,

complete with security, love and just a touch of excitement. My parents modeled a near-perfect marriage, rarely arguing. From a young age, I knew I wanted a marriage just like theirs when I grew up — one full of tenderness and loyalty. My mother devoted herself to us as a full-time homemaker, while my father provided a steady income. My home always felt like a warm blanket, wrapped snugly around my shoulders. No matter what rattled the outside world, I knew I could find security and safety inside those walls.

Church was an integral part of our lives. My parents relied on a strong faith in God, as did my grandparents. My grandparents modeled a wonderful Christian life, caring for others, praying, reading the Bible and sharing God's love with others. Awanas, Pioneer Girls, children's choir and Vacation Bible School made up just a few of my favorite church activities. When my cousin came home from Vacation Bible School one afternoon and announced she'd asked Jesus into her heart, I decided I wanted to do the same.

"You can't have what I have unless you ask Jesus in your heart yourself," she'd explained.

I wasn't about to miss out. Though just 4 years old, I'd already heard plenty about Jesus in church, and I wanted him for myself. I prayed, inviting him into my heart. As a postscript, I added, "And please, Jesus, let me be Dorothy when I grow up!" *The Wizard of Oz* had become a favorite movie of mine, and I dreamed about someday becoming Dorothy, skipping down the yellow brick road in a blue and white gingham dress and bouncy pigtails. But meeting Jesus was even more exciting than meeting the Wizard of Oz, and I could hardly wait to see where that road led.

Jesus didn't turn me into Dorothy, but I did get my chance to shine on the stage. I began dance lessons and enjoyed performing. As I got a bit older, I participated in school musicals and even landed a few speaking parts. My father loved to perform, too. He had an amazing singing voice and often took us to various churches, where he sang and shared his life story before a captivated audience. I proudly sat beside my mother as he belted out the songs. My mother, nervous, held her breath until he successfully hit the final high note. Later, my father and I sang together at the father/daughter banquet at church. As I glanced out at the sea of familiar faces, my heart surged with joy at the idea of being able to sing in unison with my beloved father.

Life off the stage was pretty great, too. My brother and I loved playing outside in the backyard, spending hours climbing trees. We returned to the house covered in sticky sap, and my mother desperately tried to scrub it off our clothes and skin. My father built us a playhouse, and we painted it as a family. My brother and I often camped out in the playhouse, joined by our sweet family dog. Camping trips to the mountains provided many lasting memories as well. When an unexpected rainstorm threatened to ruin our fun, we made the best of things and kept a sense of humor. Trips to Disneyland also proved lots of fun. My mother took a picture of my brother and me in the same spot every year to mark how much we'd grown. Life, it seemed, was one grand adventure, and I soaked it all up, ready to embrace whatever came my way.

In my latter elementary school years, my parents announced we were moving to Plano, Texas. I didn't know much about Texas, but I was pretty sure lots of cowboys lived there. I imagined owning my own horse, galloping off into the sunset in a pair of shiny leather boots. But when we arrived, there were no horses or boots — just a lump in my throat and the sting of loneliness. The girls in my class seemed to have all the right clothes, and I suddenly felt terribly out of place. I missed my friends back home and longed for the days of Disneyland rides and backyard playhouses. Innocent afternoons of climbing trees were behind me, replaced by looming adolescence and awkward changes to come.

High school brought with it many highs and lows. Though I was not popular by any means, I had plenty of friends in a variety of circles. I joined choir and made the drill team, which proved an unforgettable experience. Friday night football became the highlight of our week. My team and I worked hard to perfect our routine each day after school, enjoying the thrill of the performance as it played out under the bright lights on the field. After each game, we all headed over to IHOP and hung out until curfew. Several of my friends partied, but being a good church girl, I shied away from that scene. I listened as they gabbed about the previous weekend's antics, confused by some of their inside jokes. But I didn't feel left out. My parents had raised me with values, and I wasn't interested in compromising them.

Choir soon lost its appeal. My choir teacher, a negative woman, never seemed pleased with my performance. One day, she berated me in front of the entire school, yelling that I'd missed my cue. I shrank, mortified by her words. I dropped out of choir and stuck with singing at church, where the only one I felt I needed to worry about pleasing was God.

Like most teenage girls, I desperately wanted a boyfriend. When a guy in my 10th grade English class paid attention to me, I happily said yes to a date. I lost interest when I learned we had next to nothing in common, and we broke up after a month. He seemed to handle the breakup well, but his friends tossed out cruel remarks when I passed them in the hall, reminding me I'd crushed his heart. Not long after, I began dating another guy. He took me to watch *Sense and Sensibility* at the movies, and I soon lost all sensibilities when he made a move on me. We kissed the whole evening, but when he tried to take things further, I refused and ended the relationship. My parents had given me a promise ring when I turned 13, reminding me to guard myself physically until marriage. I took the promise seriously.

Wanting to please my parents and God, I dated a boy from my church youth group next. I lost interest in him as well, but my parents took us to dinner, reminding me how important it was to work on our relationship. *That's a lot of pressure for a girl about to graduate high school,* I mused. I hoped to emulate my parents' loyal relationship one day, but at 18, marriage was nowhere on the horizon.

When prom rolled around, I learned none of the boys I liked wanted to ask me because they knew I was a "good girl." Unlike many of the other partying girls, I would not give them what they wanted at the end of the night. Their rejection stung, but I held my ground. An old friend from another school invited me, and he treated me with respect.

High school graduation arrived at last. I was relieved to have survived in spite of the relational rollercoaster. Since transitioning to Texas, something had shifted in my heart. The moment I'd walked onto my new campus, the innocence and security I'd once known disappeared, replaced by a subtle feeling of inferiority. *You are not worthy,* the nagging voice whispered. *You are not enough.* I knew my parents loved me, and I was pretty sure God loved me, too. I had racked up an impressive resume of accomplishments since my youth. But the girl who danced across the stage, smiling, sequined and singing before the crowd, was slowly withering inside.

Two of my close girlfriends suggested we check out Texas A&M-Corpus Christi, a beach college with onsite dorms. The idea of embarking on an adventure in another city with my friends seemed exciting, and I agreed to it.

"We can be roommates! It will be so fun!" my friends and I squealed.

But shortly after settling into our dorms, I discovered college life wasn't so fun after all. My friends wanted to party all the time, and I wasn't into that scene. I sat at home watching reruns on TV, while they slipped into cute clothes and headed out for the night.

"Looks like the good church girl is staying home again tonight," my friends moaned.

"I'm fine," I assured them, curling up on the couch. But inside, I wasn't fine. The next morning, when my friends exchanged tales of drunken escapades, I felt left out and alone.

If you can't beat 'em, join 'em, I concluded at last. *I may be a good girl with values, but I'm not about to sit back and watch everyone enjoy the college life while I sit in front of the TV. I'll just go check these parties out, but I won't drink.*

It didn't take long to realize that being the only sober person at a party wasn't much fun. I began partying hard along with my peers, throwing back a few drinks in red Solo cups. Soon, the beliefs I'd clung to so tightly since my youth took a backseat, as I let loose for the first time in my life.

One night, after a party wound down at 2 a.m., I stumbled to a friend's car, only to learn it was already packed to the brim.

"I can take you home," a tall, dark-haired guy interjected.

I glanced up. *I've seen this guy around campus. He seems sweet and harmless. And sober.* "Thanks," I muttered, trying to collect myself. "I appreciate that."

The guy introduced himself as Chris. We stopped for tacos on the way home and chatted. When I spoke, he leaned in, genuinely interested in my words. *Unlike my so-called girlfriends, who left me to go partying, this guy really acts like I matter. He's a real gentleman.*

Chris drove me home, and our eyes locked again. I knew it wouldn't be the last we'd be seeing of each other.

I came down with mononucleosis shortly after and could not finish the semester. I went home to rest and returned in January, just in time to start school again. To my delight, I bumped into Chris again. One evening, I came back to my apartment to find two boxes on my bed. I opened the first one and discovered several beautiful long-stemmed roses inside. As I slid open the second box, I sucked in my breath. There sat a gorgeous dress in my size, accompanied by a note: "Be ready at 7 p.m."

I'd seen the dress at the store I worked at and had fallen in love with it. I'd mentioned it to my friend but had no idea Chris was plotting something behind the scenes. My heart jumped in my chest as I slipped on the dress. It fit perfectly. *Wow, I can't believe he went to all this trouble! This guy is a real keeper!*

Chris and I began dating, and I quickly fell in love with him. He put me right at ease and made me feel like the center of the universe. Despite my strong feelings for him, I remained adamant about maintaining my virginity. But Chris began to put the pressure on. One night, after dating for more than a year, we attended a graduation party for a friend. I began casually chatting with another guy, and Chris grew furious. Back at his apartment, he unleashed on me.

"You were flirting with that guy at the party!" he cried.

"No, I wasn't," I insisted. "He's just a friend."

Chris' eyes bore into mine. "Look, if you love me, you need to prove it. You need to give it up to me."

I gulped, knowing exactly what he had in mind. *He's right,* I decided. *I can't keep withholding sex from him. It's time I show him I really love him.*

We purchased protection at the nearest convenience store, and that night, I gave myself away, turning my heart and body over to a guy I thought I trusted and adored. Immediately, I regretted the decision. When I went home, I broke down and told my mother what I'd done.

"I'm so sad for you, but I'm not surprised," she said, tears in her eyes. "You let those two awful girlfriends of yours break you down, honey."

My chest tightened at her words. I knew she was right. I'd traded my good-girl values for a few drunken nights and cheap sex, all because I wanted to be loved. The old message, *You're not worthy,* continued to play through my mind like a record on repeat. *Why couldn't I just stand up for myself and do the right thing?*

Looking for a more wholesome approach to life, I threw myself into school activities and became president of my sorority. Chris and I continued dating, and he continued demanding much of my time. Eventually, I moved into his apartment, where I waited on him day and night. I cooked all his meals, making breakfast sausage on his George Foreman grill every morning. A very active tennis player, Chris liked hearty meals, but he always snuck in a few cigarettes, too. I convinced myself we were in love, that this was just the sort of thing devoted girlfriends did for their man.

My sorority friends encouraged me to spend time away from Chris. "Come out with us," they urged me. "Stop spending so much time with that guy. You're letting him absorb all your time."

One evening, we watched the movie *Charlie's Angels*. As I watched three tough girls fight bad guys, something stirred inside me.

"You know, you have the power to leave him," one of my friends said, turning to me.

"Why would I leave him?" I shot back.

"You're a mess. You're missing class and other activities because he's so controlling. Don't you see what he's doing to you?"

I flinched. "You're right," I agreed, nodding. "I can start standing up for myself."

I returned to Chris' apartment and told him how I felt. "I think it's healthy to do our own things sometimes," I told him, mustering a newfound strength. "I like spending time with you, but I think we can be apart, too."

Chris nodded. I knew my boldness surprised him, but I firmly held my ground. We continued dating, but I kept my boundaries. He graduated and moved away, and for the first time in a long while, I enjoyed my freedom, realizing I could breathe on my own. At last, I knew what I needed to do. I called Chris and broke up with him over the phone.

"I need to be with a guy who shares my same faith in God," I insisted. "You're welcome to go to church with me, but I'm not changing my mind."

Chris agreed to go to church and told me he'd prayed and invited God into his life. I was glad for him but didn't want to be controlled by him anymore. "I'm happy you made that decision, but we are done," I said, summoning a firm but gentle tone. "I'm happy with my life right now, and I can't be with you anymore."

Chris called for a couple more months, but I held my ground. Eventually, I stopped hearing from him. Relief flooded me, followed by a sense of empowerment. *I am not a doormat. I can be courageous and strong. I do not need a guy to make me happy. I am my own person.*

But before long, I grew lonely again. I moved back to Dallas to be near my family. A guy named Eric came along, and we began dating. Short in stature and quiet in nature, he seemed opposite of Chris in every way. Eric loved running, something I loathed, but I pretended to like it, plastering a smile on my face and breathing through my side cramps as we hit the pavement every weekend together. Eric didn't believe in God, and when we began sleeping together, I knew I'd compromised my standards. After a couple months, we went our separate ways.

One day, my aunt in California called out of the blue. She was dying in a hospital bed, ravaged by the effects of multiple myeloma. I went out to visit her and say my goodbyes. When I stepped into the room, I nearly gasped, startled by her emaciated frame. But despite her pale complexion and withered features, I saw an unusual glow radiating through her, like sunlight dancing on water.

"I want to let you know I've been talking to Jesus," my aunt said, smiling at me. "And Jesus doesn't want you to feel guilty anymore. Jesus wants you to get over the shame of being with those two boys."

Stunned, I broke down in tears. *How did she know about my boyfriends?*

Though I'd come to comfort my aunt, it was she who comforted me instead. She and my uncle prayed over me, addressing my feelings of self-worth. "You are worthy and loved," they reminded me. "Jesus wants you to know you are highly valued and cherished."

As I wiped my tears, my heart surged with joy. I couldn't remember the last time I'd been filled with such peace. The old voices that had haunted me for so long disappeared, replaced by another voice: Jesus'. Since inviting him into my heart at a young age, I had looked to him for guidance and strength. But feelings of self-loathing had subtly plagued me, and out of my brokenness and insecurity, I had traded my values for counterfeit love and acceptance. Now, I was 4 years old again, back to the innocence, the passion I had for loving Jesus reignited. The simple truth now trumped everything else: Jesus loved me, flaws and all. He had forgiven me for the wrong things I'd done, embracing me in his arms, reminding me I did not have to perform to please him. I was his, and nothing would ever change that.

I returned to church and encouraged my brother to go with me. We attended the singles group, where I skeptically glanced around, convinced everyone might be a bit weird. But to my pleasant surprise, everyone was friendly and normal.

A short, dark-haired guy with a great smile greeted me at the door and introduced himself as Drew. We began chatting, and as the weeks passed, he tried to get my brother and me more involved in the group.

"Hey, would you be interested in co-leading a Bible study?" Drew asked one day.

I blinked, surprised but pleased at his suggestion. "Sure," I replied.

"Great!" Drew beamed, flashing his mega-watt smile again. "Want to meet me at the Christian bookstore and pick out some materials?"

"Sure."

We headed to the bookstore, where I began rifling through a selection of books. As I glanced up at Drew, my heart began to pound. *No, no, stop it! What is this all about?* I flushed, feeling silly for having such feelings. *I just met this guy! I can't like him already!*

The next night, Drew and I hung out at the apartment I shared with my brother.

"I had fun last night," he said.

"Me, too," I replied. "Hey, what do we do if we have feelings for each other?" I took a deep breath as I said the words. *Might as well just put it out there, see if he's on the same page.*

"Yeah, what do we do if we have *more* feelings for each other?" Drew returned.

My heart fluttered in my chest. *Oh, wow. Okay, so this wasn't just in my head. There is something there. Now what?*

Drew and I began hanging out, getting to know each other better. We swapped stories of our pasts. I told him about the guys I'd dated. He, in turn, confided that he'd been in many sexually active relationships but that he wanted to remain pure going forward.

"My stepdad exposed me to porn when I was a little kid," Drew explained. "He would put on porn while my mom cooked dinner sometimes. My stepdad also explained sexual stuff in explicit detail to me. It was just always around. I didn't know any better."

His words came as a bit of a shock, as my parents had modeled more modest behavior. *His past doesn't matter,* I reminded myself. *Drew is a good guy and loves God. We've all messed up, but the important thing is, we've learned from our mistakes and moved on.*

On New Year's Eve, Drew and I decided to attend a get-together with our singles group. He picked me up at my apartment, and when he set his coat down, a ring fell out of the pocket. My heart skipped a beat as I spotted it. It strongly resembled one we'd eyed at the store not long before. *I know we were joking about that ring, but is he really serious? Is he going to propose? We've only been dating six weeks, but I know he's the guy for me. If he proposes, I'll say yes for sure.*

After the singles get-together, we headed back to Drew's sister's house, where he sat me in his grandmother's rocking chair. Suddenly, Drew took my hand, knelt in front of his entire family and blurted, "Will you spend the rest of your life with me?"

"Yes!" I cried.

He slipped the ring with the little blue stone on my finger, and his family erupted into celebratory noise with party poppers. His sister wandered into the room with a bouquet of white roses to welcome me into the family. Overwhelmed by joy, I could not wipe the smile off my face.

I laughed, remembering how I'd once told my brother never to propose to a girl in front of his family. Now, I could not think of a more appropriate place to celebrate our love. *I feel so embraced by their acceptance. I could not ask for a better guy or a better group of people to surround myself with. This really is the beginning of a fairytale.*

Drew and I enjoyed a whirlwind engagement and married on a muggy July afternoon that year. I could hardly wait to begin our life together, dreaming of all the things any newlywed does — babies, a new home, vacations and perhaps even a white picket fence. Little did I know the fairytale I'd envisioned would turn into a nightmare just a few short months later.

"Nooo!" I wasn't sure if the words actually escaped my throat or stuck there as they came out. I stared down at the laptop screen, suddenly afraid I might vomit. *How could he do this to me? How could my own husband betray me like this?*

Drew and I had moved into a new house, and my parents had come over to help us unpack. It was just after midnight as my mother and I finished tackling the kitchen. I wandered into the other room to find Drew and discovered him asleep, his laptop on his chest. When I glanced down, I saw pornographic images on the screen. My heart sank, and I felt as if I'd been tossed out of the rink after a bloody boxing match. My worst fears had just been confirmed before my very eyes.

I fled to the laundry room, where my screams turned into sobs. Drew jolted out of his sleep, and my mother rushed to his side, berating him over what he'd done.

"What are you thinking, son? How could you do something like this? This is awful, Drew. Very disappointing," my mother yelled.

A mixture of anger and embarrassment overwhelmed me at once. *My own parents have caught my husband in a disgusting act! This truly is my worst nightmare! What am I going to do now? How can I walk out of this room and face them all?*

After my tears subsided, I walked out of the room, but I avoided Drew's eyes for the rest of the night. Too hurt to speak, I fell into bed, praying sleep would whisk me away from the pain.

A New Song in My Heart

The next morning, we went to church. When the elders passed the communion plate, I watched in disgust as Drew took the bread. *How can he take communion right now, when he was looking at porn just a few hours before? Who does he think he is?*

Just a couple months after marrying Drew, I'd discovered the unthinkable — my new husband had a pornography addiction. I caught him viewing porn on the computer, and he confided he had a problem. The rollercoaster ride then began. Drew admitted that he had been addicted to porn for years, that his early exposure to such things had led him toward unhealthy behaviors. I recalled the first few times we'd been intimate together, how he'd seemed especially domineering and aggressive. *I just assumed he really wanted to be with me,* I thought sadly. *Now I'm afraid maybe he has a real problem. And I'm not sure what to do about it.*

I became an expert sleuth, always checking the history on Drew's computer and making sure he wasn't messing up. He insisted he wanted to change but didn't know how. I felt sick, wondering how he could fill his mind with such foul images when he had a wife who loved him. *I know you led me to him, God. So why is he doing this? I can never measure up to these beautiful women he's looking at. Doesn't he know how much it hurts me, how unwanted and unattractive this makes me feel?*

Drew and I flung hurtful words back and forth at each other. "You're a liar, and you broke your vows!" I screamed at him.

When Drew was offered a sales job in the Austin area, we drove down to check it out. As I saw rolling hills up ahead, I breathed a sigh of relief. "This reminds me of California," I told Drew happily. "I've always wanted to live in the hills. I can do this."

Drew and I moved into a new house in the Austin area, hoping to put the past behind us. *A fresh start,* I told myself hopefully. *A new job, a change of scenery. Surely, things will get better.*

But they did not. At least not right away.

After discovering Drew watching porn again, I began contemplating divorce. Our two-year anniversary was just around the corner, a milestone that should have been cause for celebration. But I didn't much feel like celebrating anymore. Three of my friends were divorcing, and it didn't seem like the end of the world. *They're moving on with their lives. Maybe I should, too. I love my husband, but I can't go on this way, not trusting him.* I listened to a popular Christian psychologist discuss tough love on the radio. He encouraged listeners to make people accountable for their actions and not let their poor decisions ruin relationships. *Okay, that's it!* I concluded. *If this guy says it's okay to leave, then I'm out!*

I waited until the next time I caught Drew watching porn, and then I pounced on him like a lion on its prey. "It's either this porn or me!" I shot at him. "I'm not doing this anymore!" But even as the words spilled out of my mouth, I cringed.

What am I doing? I don't really mean it! Drew is my best friend, and I don't want to live without him. There has to be a better way.

We found a pornography support group, and Drew agreed to go. He met with an accountability partner, who made sure he kept on track. *At last, someone besides me to keep tabs on him. Maybe we're finally making progress here!*

Meanwhile, Drew and I began trying to have a baby. I decided that a baby was the answer to our problems. Surely, an adorable little one would bring us closer together. I stopped taking birth control pills, hopeful I'd get pregnant right away. But when each month passed and I still did not conceive, I grew worried. *What's wrong with me? Am I not meant to have a baby?*

At last, in September 2006, I learned the wonderful news. Drew and I were going to be parents! As I stared at the little white stick with the two pink lines, my heart leapt with joy. *This is it! Drew and I will put the past behind us and focus on building our family.*

"Now that I'm pregnant, I want to be as healthy as possible. I'd really like to start seeing a counselor," I told Drew.

We found a Christian counselor and attended our first

session together. The counselor's stark words surprised me.

"Once trust is broken, you cannot rebuild it," the counselor told us bluntly.

I felt as if an electrical jolt had just ripped through my body. *That doesn't seem right. God talks about second chances in the Bible. We've all messed up. Is it really true that I can never learn to trust my husband again?*

"I don't want to go back there," I told Drew after our second session. "We will find someone else."

A friend whose husband had undergone an affair suggested another Christian counselor who specialized in sexual addiction. We made an appointment, and immediately, I knew we'd come to the right place. The counselor had us do several exercises, including writing letters to each other from the other's point of view. The experiment proved especially eye-opening.

"I thought you were my Prince Charming, but you deceived me," Drew wrote in my voice. "You have hurt me deeply, but I still deeply love you."

The letter moved me to tears. *Wow, Drew realizes how much he's hurt me. He doesn't want to, but he's struggling with something heavy, and he needs real help. I don't want our marriage to fail. I know we're meant to be together.*

Drew began individual counseling, where he dove deep into his past. He realized that his trigger came in the second grade, when his parents divorced. Yearning for his father's love, he tried finding that love in pornography, which his stepfather introduced him to when Drew was 10 years old. He learned to view women in an unhealthy manner instead of receiving love the right way. This led to his sexual aggression and addiction.

Slowly, I noticed a change in Drew. He softened, no longer defensive about his behavior. We began fighting less, and I learned to trust him again. I shuddered, thinking how close I'd come to filing for divorce. *That was never what I wanted. Thank you, God, for intervening in our marriage. You are truly the restorer of all things.*

Christmastime neared, and Drew and I began decorating the house. *This time next year, our little one will have presents under the tree,* I marveled, glancing down at my belly. But weeks before Christmas, my dreams came to a screeching halt when I began spotting. I looked up the symptom in my pregnancy book and learned spotting was quite common. Drew prayed over me, and I went to bed.

The next morning, Drew met me at the doctor's office. The doctor waved the fetal heart monitor over my stomach, her face furrowing when she did not detect a heartbeat. She pressed harder, but there was only silence. My own heart thudded in my chest as I anticipated the worst. The doctor sent us in for an ultrasound, which revealed there was no baby in the sac. I stared at the dark, black hole on the screen, and a dark, black hole began to form inside me. *My baby is gone. The baby I dreamed about, the miracle baby that was supposed to bring Drew and me closer again. Gone, just like that.*

Drew hugged me tightly, and we bawled together,

mourning the child that would never open his presents under the tree. I went through the natural process of miscarriage the doctor had explained. It continued for the next couple of weeks. Drew's family came to visit, and I tried to busy myself with the usual Christmas preparations to take my mind off things. My mother-in-law and I baked peanut brittle together in the kitchen and listened to cheerful carols. But the cramping and clotting worsened, followed by a severe head rush, and I began to worry.

Two days before Christmas, I called the doctor to explain my symptoms, and she told me to meet her at the hospital right away. I could hardly function by the time Drew brought me in. The doctors performed an emergency DNC and sent me off to recovery. When I awoke, I discovered Drew at my side, his eyes flooded with concern. He cried with me, held my hand and prayed, asking God to get us through this difficult time. He then made a few jokes to lighten the mood. It was at that moment that I realized how much he truly cared for me. For the first time since learning of his addiction, I saw a man who would have jumped over the moon to save me, a man who was truly crazy about his wife, a man who did not want to lose his best friend. I had found my knight in shining armor.

The following June, Drew and I took a two-day trip to Disneyland to celebrate our third anniversary. When we got back to the hotel, I noticed a strange sore under my arm, but I brushed it off as an ingrown hair from shaving. The following day, I began feeling especially faint and nauseous. I tried to keep up with Drew as we made our rounds inside the park, but by lunchtime, I completely fell apart.

"Maybe you just need to eat," Drew concluded. He grabbed me some lunch, but the smells made me so nauseous that I raced to the bathroom instead. Sweat poured out of me as I leaned against the bathroom wall, basking in its coolness. *What is wrong with me? I'm a total mess!*

I returned to Drew. "I'm not well. We need to leave right now," I insisted.

At a family gathering that night, I struggled to hold it together, feeling worse by the minute. I asked my mother to take a look at my underarm, and she completely panicked as she glanced down.

"What?" I asked, panicking as her eyes bulged. And then I saw it — a lump the size of an orange. "It was just a little bump this morning! What's going on?"

My mother told the family, and they suggested I get to the nearest doctor right away. Drew took me to the emergency room, where the doctors lanced the lump to drain it, then followed up with antibiotics.

"I'd get it checked at another ER in a couple days to make sure it's healing properly," the doctor said before we left.

The next few days of the trip were a blur as my pain worsened. A fever took over, and I grew delirious, wiping my face and neck down with a wet washcloth to cool off. Drew took me to another emergency room and asked the doctors to recheck my wound. When the nurse saw the wound, she frantically ran out of the room.

"That's weird. What's going on?" I muttered.

The doctor poked his head in the door a minute later. "The infectious disease specialist is being paged," he informed me.

Infectious disease specialist? That doesn't sound good! Someone, tell me what's going on!

I soon learned the truth. I had MRSA, a strain of staph infection resistant to standard antibiotics. The doctor admitted me to the hospital under quarantine and proceeded to administer strong antibiotics.

"Do you think we could run a pregnancy test, just to make sure I'm not pregnant?" I asked. Drew and I hadn't been trying for a baby, but we hadn't exactly been preventing a pregnancy, either.

The nurse returned a few minutes later, smiling. "Guess what? You're pregnant!" she announced.

Drew and I glanced at each other and began laughing and crying simultaneously. *This is certainly great news, but it could not have come at a more horrible time!*

Fear gripped me over the next few days as I remained in the hospital. *What if we lose this child, too?* I prayed, asking God for comfort. Drew remained by my side, crying, praying and laughing with me as the irony hit us both. *I have something terribly life-threatening and dangerous living inside of me, but I also have something wonderful and magical living inside me, too. Please, God, watch over our little one.*

After three days, the doctors discharged me and sent me home with IV antibiotics, which Drew had to administer to me. *My salesman husband is now a nurse with no medical training,* I mused. *I sure hope he knows what he's doing!*

When at last we returned home, I scheduled a visit with my obstetrician, where I saw our baby on the ultrasound screen for the first time. *Wow, it looks just like a little peanut,* I marveled. *Another miracle baby. Thank you, God!*

Sickness plagued me every day of the pregnancy, but I embraced it, knowing I was growing a healthy baby inside. As my belly swelled, I gave myself permission to celebrate. Drew and I counted down the days until our little one arrived.

In November that year, I read the novel *Redeeming Love* by Francine Rivers, a story of a man who obeyed God's call to marry a woman sold into prostitution. Angel was an embittered young woman with a hardened heart, but Michael Hosea never stopped pursuing her with his love. Even when Angel ran from his embrace, Michael kept loving her. At last, Angel learned to trust in the love that mattered most — God's.

Though not an especially avid reader, I could not put the book down. As I came to the last pages, I began sobbing. *God, you have given Drew to me as a gift, and I have rejected him. I stopped wanting to divorce him long ago, but I have not truly embraced the wonderful man you've given to me. I'm so sorry.*

I went to Drew and did something out of the ordinary — I proposed to him. "Now that I know everything about you, I feel I need to ask you to marry me … again," I said with a smile.

Drew accepted my proposal, and we decided to renew our vows after the baby was born. From that moment on, I knew I'd never take him for granted again.

A month before my due date, my blood pressure suddenly climbed. The doctor prescribed bed rest and diagnosed preeclampsia, a dangerous condition. A few days later, I went into labor. As the doctor instructed me to push, I laughed, and our precious little Jake came right out. A healthy 6 pounds, 3 ounces, he was perfect in every way. Drew and I marveled at his tiny features, unable to believe that after all our struggles, our precious baby was here at last.

Within the first few days, I noticed Jake wasn't gaining weight. The doctors diagnosed him with jaundice and almost diagnosed him with failure to thrive, but they soon discovered the root of his struggles. Jake had an extra-tightened piece of skin under his tongue and could not touch the roof of his mouth, making it difficult to swallow. The doctors performed a simple but painful procedure, and within no time, he gained weight and turned into a plump, happy baby. I resigned from my teaching job to stay home with him full time, diving headfirst into motherhood.

On July 3, the same day as our original wedding date, Drew and I renewed our vows in a simple backyard ceremony. I wore a casual sundress, and we both went barefoot, just like we'd always wanted to do. Pork chops and green beans made up the reception menu. It was a perfectly beautiful day, even more meaningful than our first wedding. After enduring so much, I finally appreciated my wonderful husband just as he was. We had endured triumph and tragedy, and in the end, we'd emerged stronger, our faith in each other and in God renewed.

Drew and I had been searching for a new church for some time. One weekend, while I was away visiting family, Drew visited Believers Church in nearby Leander. He called me after the service ended.

"I really enjoyed it. Everyone seems passionate about God, and I got a really good feeling," he said excitedly.

When I returned, I visited with him and instantly knew we'd found a place to call home. "I think we have a church," I said, tears filling my eyes. "This is it."

Drew and I got involved with various activities at Believers Church and enjoyed the genuine people we met. If they said they were praying for us, I knew for certain they were. We performed in the Easter and Christmas plays, and I joined a women's Bible study. We also helped with Vacation Bible School and Sunday school, teaching young children about God's love just as I'd been taught as a child. *Thanks, God. Things have really come full circle. What an answer to prayer!*

In 2010, my beloved grandmother passed away. I knew I'd miss her terribly. As a child, I'd seen her at the kitchen table every morning, praying for us. When I'd gone off to college, she'd given me the Bible verse Proverbs 3:5-6 as a reminder to trust in God. "Trust in the Lord with all your heart, and lean not on your own understanding. In all your ways, submit to him and he will make your paths straight." The verse rang in my head as I said my goodbyes to her. *Oma, you lived a life of faith, and I'm forever grateful for your prayers, for I know they held me when I veered off the right path. I will see you again someday in heaven!*

In August that year, I learned I was pregnant again, but within a few weeks, I miscarried. Drew and I grieved another baby-to-be. *Maybe my body just isn't meant to carry babies,* I wondered sadly. *But the doctor convinced me to keep trying.*

In October 2011, I became pregnant again. Drew and I were elated, as we'd always wanted children close together. As the months passed and my belly grew, we breathed a sigh of relief.

My mother-in-law invited me to a women's event at her church, described as a crash course in group counseling. *I'm fine now. I've dealt with my marriage crisis, and I'm in a good place,* I convinced myself. But as I participated in the day's exercises, I realized I had not dealt with my anger at God for allowing my two babies to die. The questions suddenly came like a tidal wave, as I began yelling at him.

Why, God? Why would you give me two babies, only to take them away?

A woman approached me with some encouraging words. "God can handle your anger. It's okay to give yourself the freedom to be angry with him," she said kindly.

Relief swept over me, as I realized that God, too, was heartbroken over the loss of my babies. He had grieved along with me in my darkest hour. Knowing this helped me release the pent-up anger, and I walked away from the event lighter and freer than ever. My broken heart was healed at last.

On July 13, 2012, we welcomed a beautiful little girl, Elana, into the world. With a darling boy and perfect pink little girl, our family seemed complete.

But God was not done with us just yet. Another surprise was waiting for us just around the corner.

I stared at the pregnancy test in disbelief.

God, could it really be true?

After some health complications following Elana's birth, Drew and I had decided not to have any more children. Though we'd originally wanted a large family, the pregnancies and miscarriages had taken a toll on my body. We both felt at peace about being a family of four, but now, it appeared, we'd be expanding to five.

As the news sank in, we both grew excited, wondering if the baby would be a boy or a girl. But after just a few weeks, I began spotting. My heart dropped to the floor.

Oh, not again. I can't handle another miscarriage, God. Please, not again.

I went to the church, where a missionary had come to do a prayer service. After a few songs and a message, the missionary asked those needing prayer to come forward. *I don't really feel comfortable going forward like this, but I know I need prayer right now,* I thought, rising from my seat. I made my way forward and began bawling as I reached the front.

"Dear God, we ask that you would please heal Denise's body and fix whatever is currently wrong with it," the missionary prayed, laying hands on me.

His words sent a chill up my spine. *God, how does he know? I didn't even tell him about my pregnancy scare!*

The pastor's daughter came forward and prayed for me as well. "God, help Denise to know that her body is not broken. She is not a failure."

More tears flowed down my cheeks. *Oh, God, thank you! I believe you are healing me right now, taking care of this little baby inside my womb. Thank you!*

I went to the doctor, who confirmed through an ultrasound that my pregnancy was right on track. The spotting subsided, and a peace arose in my heart.

This baby is going to be okay. We're both going to be okay. The pregnancy may not have been planned by me, but it certainly was planned by you, God. And I know this child will be a blessing to everyone.

I told Drew the good news, and he rejoiced with me. As I gazed into the face of the man I loved, I recalled a conversation we'd had some time ago. "You know what? I wish we hadn't wasted so much time hating each other during our early years," he'd said wistfully, tears filling his eyes. "I know we still drive each other crazy sometimes, but there's no one I'd rather do life with than you."

My due date is just a few months away. I am reminded daily of the gift of new life. Like spring flowers sprouting in the dirt after a harsh winter's storm, new life offers the promise of hope. And it is through Jesus that I have found that hope.

As a young girl, I strived to be good, holding tightly to my Christian values. But a nagging voice crept in, whispering, *You are not worthy*, and it took years to silence that voice for good. After Drew's struggle with addiction, I questioned my value again, wondering if the man I'd married would ever love me unconditionally. Now, I am at peace. The world may often fail me, and people may let me down, but I have a heavenly father who accepts me as I am. He has healed me both physically and emotionally, and he has mended my broken heart. He has restored my marriage, and he has blessed me with new life. I may no longer dance on the stage before a crowd, but I still have a song in my heart, and I'm ready to share it with the world.

The encore is still to come.

A Father's Son

The Story of Jim

Written by Karen Koczwara

The horrified look in my girlfriend's eyes said it all — something terrible had happened the night before. The color drained from her face, her entire body shook and tears streamed down her cheeks as she sat crumpled in the front seat of my car. I had never seen her so distraught.

"What is it?" I pressed, growing anxious. "Tell me, now!"

At last, she managed to spit the words out. "My mother's boyfriend … he raped me last night."

"What are you talking about?" I nearly flew out of my seat. "He raped you?"

She nodded, now sobbing hysterically. "My mom got me drunk, held me down and had her boyfriend rape me."

For a moment, time stood still. I felt as if I'd been socked in the gut. My girlfriend — the love of my life — raped? And how could her mother have done such a wicked thing? It was unthinkable, the worst imaginable act. And I had not been there to stop it.

A mixture of sorrow, pity and rage filled me at once. I wanted to comfort my girlfriend, to let her know this was not her fault, to remind her it was all going to be okay. But at the same time, I wanted to find her mother and that guy and tear them to shreds with my bare hands. My blood boiled as the adrenaline surged through my veins.

The Road Leads Home

I will find them, and I will make them pay. They will not get away with this!

I was born in Oklahoma, a place where rolling hills, live music, cowboys and business entrepreneurs collide. My first few years of life were filled with normal boyish fun — riding bikes, climbing trees and playing with my brother, five years my junior. My mother stayed home with my brother and me, while my father worked in the supplied materials industry. When I turned 7, we moved to Florida and settled into a different routine. My parents' relationship took a rocky turn, and they divorced. My father found work as a bouncer at a bar on the beach, where he met a new woman. They married, and my brother and I moved back to Austin with them shortly after.

We settled in the Cedar Park area, just outside Austin. School did not come easily for me, and I struggled. At 10 years old, I began attending a small church with my father. The small church immediately felt like home, and I enjoyed my new friends there. They were the sort of folks who would show up on your doorstep in your time of need, armed with groceries, casseroles or a comforting hug.

I went around school, sharing Jesus with everyone I met. By middle school, my peers began calling me "Preacher Man."

I didn't mind the title — it seemed fitting. *Maybe I will grow up and become a preacher someday,* I mused.

I joined the football team and enjoyed the sport. But by eighth grade, everything changed. My best friend introduced me to a new group of guys, and we began hanging out with them regularly. Soon, I began smoking cigarettes. At first, it didn't seem like a big deal. All the cool guys seemed to smoke, and I figured it was harmless fun. But soon, pot entered the scene. My best friend's dad had a stash of it, and we began smoking that as well. Before long, we got our hands on other drugs, including ecstasy. I liked the way the drugs made me feel — high, happy, numb from my problems. When on drugs, I forgot all about school, my life at home and my parents' divorce. I kept God tucked away, an afterthought I figured I could pull out in an emergency someday down the road. But for now, "Preacher Man" had hung up his hat.

I continued partying throughout high school. My stepmother got pregnant, and she and my father had a daughter. Meanwhile, my mother remarried and gave birth to another boy and girl. I saw her here and there but continued living with my father. He and I had always been close, but as my partying increased, we began fighting regularly. Several of our extended family members worked in law enforcement, and my father warned me I'd better keep in line. But I wasn't interested in listening to him. I'd been lured in by booze and drugs, and they now ruled my life.

One evening, I headed out to a house party, ready for

another night of fun. There, I met a pretty girl named Kari. Short, with dark blond hair, green eyes, rosy red cheeks and a striking smile, she caught my attention right away. We struck up a conversation, and I immediately felt at ease in her presence. We stayed up all night talking, watching the sunrise as it crept over the hills the next morning. I found myself telling her about my family, and Kari told me about her tumultuous relationship with her mother. It seemed we had much in common, and by the time we parted ways, I had a hunch I'd met my soul mate.

Just two months after we began dating, I asked Kari to marry me. I wanted to be with her, she wanted to be with me and we had no qualms about our future. A month later, Kari learned she was pregnant. We were elated. We counted the days until her due date. When we discovered we were having a girl, the reality became even more exciting. I dropped out of school to get a job, while Kari carried on with her studies until the baby was due.

Kari and I moved in together. She gave birth to a healthy little girl, and we loved our new roles as parents. Though young, I felt certain we had what it took to last a lifetime. Our newborn daughter turned from a tiny infant to a plump, happy baby, and we relished her every move. But when our daughter was just 6 months old, we got into a fight.

"I'm going to stay at my mom's house!" Kari yelled, storming off.

The next morning, when I went to pick her up, she was completely distraught and disheveled. Her shoulders shook as she sobbed, and then she relayed the horrific events from the night before.

"My mother got me drunk, then held me down while her boyfriend raped me," she sputtered, hardly able to get the words out.

I felt as if I'd just taken a blow to the face and had been knocked out of the boxing ring. "They did what?" I cried, enraged. The idea was despicable. I knew Kari's mother had been cruel to her in the past, but I'd never imagined she'd do a terrible thing like this. Right then and there, I decided they were not going to get away with it. I would go to all possible lengths to have them thrown behind bars.

I called the police right away and told them the story. They assured me they'd act quickly. I then called Kari's mother.

"What were you thinking?" I screamed. "You're a sick person, and you're not going to get away with this!" I then followed with a string of angry words and expletives. My stomach churned as I slammed down the phone. *Justice will be served, you witch,* I thought to myself. *You just better watch out!*

The police soon informed me they'd caught her mother's boyfriend all the way in Alabama, where they found him running through the woods. They threw him and her mother behind bars. Because Kari was just 17 years old, Child Protective Services intervened. Her dad offered to take her in, and she was placed with him in New Braunfels, a town not far from Austin, Texas. Our young daughter stayed with me. In just a matter of days, my entire life had been torn to shreds.

I felt hopeless and helpless, pacing the floors, smoking one cigarette after another. Nothing seemed to ease my nerves. How on earth was I going to help Kari? And how could I shake these feelings of rage toward her mother and her boyfriend? They might be locked up now, but they've ruined her life — and mine! How can I ever forgive them for such a disgusting act?

One day, my father invited me to go with him to the church I'd grown up in, where he still attended. I hadn't set foot in church for some time, as I'd wandered far away from my faith. Years before, I'd enjoyed attending Sunday school and hearing about Jesus from the Bible. The message seemed simple. God loved us, he had a plan for our lives and he wanted a relationship with us so we could spend eternity with him in heaven. At 10 years old, it was all I needed to know. I had gone to church off and on over the years, but I didn't pay much attention to the message. To me, church had become nothing more than a Sunday morning ritual.

But now, everything seemed dark. I didn't know what to do or where to turn. I knew I needed something good. And I was pretty sure I might find that inside those church doors.

As I sat in the pew, I listened to the preacher read excerpts from the Bible. Suddenly, everything made perfect sense. The preacher talked about God's love, and I listened with fresh ears and an open heart. He spoke about a God who loved us unconditionally, a God who would — and had — gone to the ends of the earth to bring us into his arms. With God, we could experience the hope, peace and joy we'd been searching for our whole lives.

That morning, Jesus completely grabbed a hold of me. I had known about him for years, even preaching about him to my peers. But I had never invited him into my heart, surrendering my life to him. Now, I was ready to do just that. I knew I could not do things on my own. I needed a Savior, and that Savior was Jesus. He had come to earth as a man, paying the price for my wrongdoings by sacrificing himself on an old wooden cross. He was still alive today, pursuing me with his love. He readily accepted me just as I was, and I didn't need to wait a moment longer to begin a relationship with him.

From that day on, I laid all my burdens down at Jesus' feet. The darkness, the hopelessness, the confusion, the tragedies that had weighed on me for so long felt like they'd just disappeared. I realized that no matter what difficult circumstances came my way, I could face them because I had Jesus in my life. Jesus would fight my battles for me. I need only trust in him.

Unable to contain my excitement about Jesus, I began sharing my renewed faith in God with Kari. "I know life has been hard, but our struggles on this earth are just temporary," I told her. "Jesus died on the cross for the wrong things we've done so we could spend eternity with him in heaven. If we surrender our lives to him, we can enjoy a relationship with him on earth and for the rest of our lives. He promises to wipe away every tear and make everything right someday."

Kari sensed the shift in me. "I can tell you really are a changed person," she said. "I want to know more about Jesus."

As Kari and I continued to talk, we discussed the horrific act her mother and boyfriend had committed. Though they were both behind bars, the incident was still fresh in our minds and hearts. However, as I came to understand Jesus' love, I gained a new perspective on the tragic incident. I realized that we were all broken people in need of forgiveness. None of us would live a perfect life. We would all hurt people and be hurt as well. It was all part of the messy, evil world we lived in. Satan, God's enemy, came to destroy and kill, but Jesus came to give life. The evil things in the world were not from God but from Satan. Jesus, however, offered everlasting life. The hurtful things we experienced broke his heart, too. He came to restore, and by asking for forgiveness, and forgiving those who had hurt us, we could experience that full restoration in our hearts.

I chose to forgive Kari's mother and boyfriend. Forgiving them did not mean letting them off the hook for the horrific act they committed. It simply meant turning the situation over to God so I could experience peace in my own heart. The moment I chose to forgive them, I felt lighter, as if the backpack of bricks I'd been carrying around had been lifted from my shoulders. What a wonderful feeling of freedom!

As I forgave them, I realized I, too, needed to ask God for forgiveness. I recalled the harsh words I'd flung at Kari's mother in a fit of rage.

God, I'm sorry for saying such horrible things. I have your spirit in me now, and I don't want to act like that anymore. Please forgive me.

I began attending church regularly, soaking up every word the preacher said. I also began reading my Bible regularly, unable to get enough of God's word. It felt wonderful to return to being the hopeful boy of my youth, the boy who'd discovered Jesus in that small church and instantly fallen in love with him.

I'd tried living life my way, partying with a bad crowd, doing drugs and drinking. The lifestyle had lured me in, seemingly fun at first, but it had proven empty. I no longer needed any of that stuff because I had something much more fulfilling — a lasting, authentic relationship with Jesus.

My father noticed a change in me, and I thanked God for mending a bond that had once been broken. I read a Bible story about someone called the prodigal son, and it resonated with me. A son had gone out into the world, turning his back on family and God to live a life of partying and self-destruction. At last, weary, empty and lonely, the son had sheepishly returned home, hoping his family would take him back. To his delight, his father met him with open arms, embracing the wayward son as though no time had passed at all. Then, the father threw him a lavish party, complete with all the finest food. The story brought tears to my eyes, as I realized that not only had my heavenly father welcomed me into his arms, but my earthly father had as well.

"I am so proud of you, son," my father said, relaying the words every boy longs to hear his father say.

Kari returned to the Austin area, and we continued to grow in our new relationship with God. Wanting to be right before God and eager to resume our life together, we decided to marry. A pastor at a small local church offered to perform the nuptials in his church office. We exchanged vows in a simple ceremony, and I looked forward to spending the rest of my life with her. Meanwhile, I prayed about finding a better job. I had been holding a temporary job at a water plant, but the government did not officially open the position for me. When no other full-time work turned up, I worried I might have to resort to working for minimum wage at a fast-food restaurant.

"I'll do whatever it takes to provide for Kari and our daughter, but I pray that if you have something better for me, God, you will please give me the opportunity. I trust in you."

One of my friends at church told my stepmother about a job opening for a truck driver, and I called the head of the company to discuss the position. He offered me the job, and I was elated. I would now have a full-time truck route, installing safety railings for houses and delivering wooden staircases. It was a job I would not only enjoy, but one that would amply provide for my family.

Thank you, God! I trusted in you, and you provided. You are so faithful!

I frequented a Christian bookstore, where I befriended a kind older woman, Emily. Emily and I frequently talked about God, and one day, she invited me to Believers Church, where she attended. I began to pray about it, feeling God might be leading us there. Kari prayed as well, and she felt even more strongly that we needed to attend. We made the move and were immediately glad we did. The church felt like home from the minute we walked in the doors, and I knew we'd found a place to raise our family and grow in our relationship with God. Believers Church was a place for everyone, a place where folks from all walks of life could find unconditional love, friendship and support. I had a hunch we'd be there for a very long time.

"I like that song. Play it again."

Kari smiled at me as I set down my guitar. I smiled back, glancing down at her growing belly. In just a few months, we'd introduce another little girl to our family. A sibling for our daughter — another life to nurture. I could not wait to meet our new baby.

Since inviting Jesus into my heart, I have completely turned my life around. I even stopped smoking cigarettes several months ago, and it feels wonderful to finally snuff out a bad habit I held onto for so long. I now rely on God's strength for everything, knowing nothing is impossible with him. Even when life feels overwhelming, bleak or just plain hard, I can rely on him.

Kari and I are now both faithfully serving God, active at Believers Church, where we attend regularly. I am grateful for a church that, like my father, has welcomed me with open arms. They have become a second family to me, and I know that if a tragedy should occur, they would be the first ones on our doorstep, offering encouragement, love and support.

I sometimes play my guitar in the church band as well. As a teen, I loved playing music and even recorded an acoustic country music CD when I was 16. But the music I write today is quite different than the music I wrote back then. I now play music for Jesus, giving him all the glory as I sing.

My job has allowed me to provide for our growing family so Kari can stay home with our children. Today, we enjoy spending time together, hanging out at church and taking walks in the beautiful parks in the Austin area. I thank God every day for his provision.

As I think back on the horrific incident that occurred in Kari's life, I realize circumstances could have been quite different. I could have let bitterness and anger fester indefinitely in my heart. But instead, Jesus got a hold of me, and he changed me radically from the inside out. Through him, Kari and I were able to forgive her mother and boyfriend. We both hope and pray they will someday come to know the Jesus we know, the one who wipes away every tear, who turns darkness to light, who brings rest to the weary and joy to the lost. There is no one too broken or dirty for God. He can use anyone, no matter what he or she has done in the past. Jesus came to restore, and he has done just that in my life.

As a boy, I embraced the good news of Jesus' love and my peers' nickname for me, "Preacher Man." But life got tough, and I lost my way. I was the wayward prodigal son. Today, however, I am a new man. I have a heavenly father who loves me, and I am his beloved son.

I have come home for good.

Conclusion

I was seated in the middle of a circular classroom, about halfway up the incline of the student seating, listening to a guest lecture by Dr. Jack Rosell. My major at Northwest University required a psychology class, and so there I was, somewhat bored, nodding off. My ears perked up when I heard the following words: *"People can change, and no one needs to remain stuck in a place with no hope."* Dr. Rosell went on to explain that with God's grace (his unmerited favor), anyone and everyone had an opportunity to experience a transformation that ultimately leads to a better life.

I asked myself the question: "Is it true? Can people really be changed?" The overwhelming evidence points to an absolute conclusion. "Yes, people can change!" A friend of mine works in a program called Teen Challenge. It deals with people who have had their lives torn up by drug and alcohol addiction. A few years ago, they started showing (with the permission of the participants in the program) before and after pictures. The transformation was incredible. The tired and worn faces of young people with no hope had morphed into faces that were bursting with health and vitality — each face, a miracle.

What does your miracle look like? What destiny does God have in mind for you? Can your life really change? You have just read seven stories that affirm what I know to be true — *"People can change, and no one needs to remain stuck in a place with no hope!"* The stories you have read are only the tip of the iceberg of lives that have been rescued by the love of God.

I think that a lot of people have the wrong notion about church people. It is commonly thought that people who go to church must either "have it all together" or must really be "good" people. On the other hand, church people are accused of being hypocrites. I think church people could only be accurately pegged as hypocrites if they actually believe that they "have it all together" or are really "good." Most of "us" church people actually have a more accurate view of the truth … that truth being that we are in need of God's help.

Please do not wait until you think you are "good enough" to go to church — just come as you are and join the rest of us. We are just people — people who have problems, people who have struggled, people who have messed up and ultimately people who found hope and the power to change in our relationship with God.

Jesus came to earth and talked about his mission. He said, "I have come that they might have life and that more abundantly." His purpose for coming was to give all of us a better opportunity to live a life that is both blessed and a blessing to those who know us. Here is the plain truth: When Jesus is allowed into a person's heart, not only does Jesus give that individual the power to change and to live a measurably better life, the new Believer has a compelling effect on the people close to them as the love of God is revealed.

Conclusion

Marriages are restored. Self-destructive behavior is reformed. Broken lives are mended. Hope that life can be better and that people can change is demonstrated as the power of God brings transformation.

This is not the experience of a few isolated cases — it is not limited to the seven lives who shared their stories in this book — it is the experience of millions of lives that have been radically changed by the grace and mercy of God!

So ... what are you waiting for? What do you have to lose? Why not listen to the voice of God that is telling you there is hope ... that you can change! If you are unable to be with us, yet you intuitively sense you would really like to experience such a life change, here are some basic thoughts to consider. If you choose, at the end of this conclusion, you can pray the suggested prayer. If your prayer genuinely comes from your heart, you will experience the beginning stages of authentic life change, similar to those you have read about.

How does this change occur?

Recognize that what you're doing isn't working. Accept the fact that Jesus desires to forgive you for your bad decisions and selfish motives. Realize that without this forgiveness, you will continue a life separated from God and his amazing love. In the Bible, the book of Romans, chapter 6, verse 23 reads that the result of sin (seeking our way rather than God's way) is death, but the gift that God freely gives is everlasting life found in Jesus Christ.

Believe in your heart that God passionately loves you and wants to give you a new heart. Ezekiel 11:19 reads, "I will give them singleness of heart and put a new spirit within them. I will take away their stony, stubborn heart and give them a tender, responsive heart" (NLT).

Believe in your heart that "if you confess with your mouth that Jesus is Lord and believe in your heart that God raised him from the dead, you will be saved" (Romans 10:9 NLT).

Believe in your heart that because Jesus paid for your failure and wrong motives, and because you asked him to forgive you, he has filled your new heart with his life in such a way that he transforms you from the inside out. Second Corinthians 5:17 reads, "When someone becomes a Christian, he becomes a brand new person inside. He is not the same anymore. A new life has begun!"

Why not pray now?

Lord Jesus, if I've learned one thing in my journey, it's that you are God and I am not. My choices have not resulted in the happiness I hoped they would bring. Not only have I experienced pain, I've also caused it. I know I am separated from you, but I want that to change. I am sorry for the choices I've made that have hurt myself, others and denied you. I believe your death paid for my sins, and you are now alive to change me from the inside out. Would you please do that now? I ask you to come and live in me so that I can sense you are here with me. Thank you for hearing and changing me. Now please help me know when you are speaking to me, so I can cooperate with your efforts to change me. Amen.

Leander's unfolding story of God's love is still being written … and your name is in it.

I hope to see you this Sunday!

RJ Dugone
Believers Church
Leander, Texas

We would love for you to join us at Believers Church!

We meet Sunday mornings at 10 a.m. at
1650 Country Road 270, Leander, TX 78641.

Please call us at 512.773.5392 for directions,
or contact us at www.believerschurchleander.com.

For more information on reaching your city with stories from your church, go to www.testimonybooks.com.

Good Catch Publishing

Did one of these stories touch you?
Did one of these real people move you to tears?
Tell us (and them) about it on our Facebook page at www.facebook.com/GoodCatchPublishing.